Starting a Garden or Landscape Business

Starting a Garden or Landscape Business

John Mason

Dip.Hort.Sc., Supn Cert., Adv.Cert.App.Mgt.

Kangaroo Press

EDITORIAL ASSISTANTS

Staff of the Australian Correspondence Schools, including:
Iain Harrison Dip.Hort.Sc.
Kathy Travis B.Sc.Ag., Ass.App.Sc, Grad.Dip.Bus, Perm.Des.Cert.
Paul Plant B.App.Sc.(Hort)

Some sections of this book have been adapted from articles and course notes, with permission from the Australian Correspondence Schools.

STARTING A GARDEN OR LANDSCAPE BUSINESS

First published in Australia and New Zealand in 1998 by Kangaroo Press
an imprint of Simon & Schuster Australia
20 Barcoo Street, East Roseville NSW 2069

A Viacom Company
Sydney New York London Toronto Tokyo Singapore

© John Mason 1998

National Library of Australia
Cataloguing-in-Publication data

Mason, John. 1951-

Includes index.

ISBN 0 86417 957 X

1. Landscaping industry - Australia - Management. 2. New business enterprises - Australia - Management 3. Small business - Australia - Management 4. Gardening - Australia - Management I. Title

712.0681

Set in Palatino 9.3

Printed by Australian Print Group, Maryborough, Victoria

10 9 8 7 6 5 4 3 2 1

Contents

I
Getting Started

The first decade of my working life was spent learning about business. The second decade was spent using what I had learnt. Now, as I enter my third decade in the workforce, I find myself with a series of profitable business interests that have a growth rate above the inflation rate and a structure that affords me a degree of financial and personal flexibility I would never have had working for someone else.

For me, success in business has been attained by following some simple guidelines, and keeping a balance between the attention given to each one. It is all too easy to concentrate on one 'rule' and ignore the others. No matter how important that rule is, sooner or later your business will come unstuck because some other 'rule' or guideline has been neglected.

SETTING YOUR COURSE

I believe your business has a greatly increased chance of success if you follow the guidelines that have kept me on course. They are:

1. Don't rush it

Businesses which try to do too much too soon have a far greater chance of eventual failure, even if they are initially successful. It is wise to devise a thorough business plan before starting up, and to have a long-term plan (10 to 20 years) that you can slowly work towards. In my case, I was setting up a correspondence school. I saw that the first step was to establish a reputable name and I considered that to do so might take many years. Hence for the first five years, I was not impatient about making money—I made sure that I had other sources of income apart from my school. It was more important at that stage to gain acceptance and recognition amongst potential 'customers' than to make a profit.

This sort of plan will generally require you to put in quite a few extra hours of work, juggling your time between raising a living and trying to develop your new business. However, in the long term, if your business becomes a success you should have greater opportunities for relaxation, hobbies and other personal interests.

2. Offer something in short supply

Your chances of success will increase greatly if you can supply something people want but can't easily get elsewhere. A lot can be gained by taking time to study the way people live, the things they do in their day-to-day lives and the problems they encounter.

Many businesses have been based on the observation that in modern society, where both husband and wife work, it is a problem for the family to find time to get the mundane day-to-day chores done. Consider the rapid increase in recent years of child-minding services, lawnmowing businesses and fast-food chains. All provide ways to get essential things done more easily for people who have the money but don't have the time.

You do not necessarily have to come up with a new concept—if, for example, you live in a rural area where goods and services that are readily available in larger cities are scarce or not available, you might be able to establish a valuable business providing one or more of these items.

Get to know your market. Research plays a very important part in choosing what goods or services to supply. This might involve looking in newspapers and magazines to see what sort of goods and services are lacking in your area and noting what is successful in other areas, but hasn't yet been tried in yours. Market research does not need to be formal. It can be based on observations of what is happening and what people want, and aligning your strengths to the gap in the market.

Taking heed of your own observations or needs can be an excellent way of finding a niche area that could be filled. For example, a lady in Melbourne was concerned about sunburn on her bare right arm when driving. She obtained some fabric with a high sun protection factor and, after experimenting with a few designs, created a simple pull-on sleeve to go over the bare right arm of a car driver. Other people expressed interest in her designs, and she began to make and sell them to friends and acquaintances. Word of mouth from these customers created more sales. She began to advertise a little, sold her product through selected shops, and soon she was producing larger amounts in different sizes and a variety of colours. Several chain stores expressed interest or began to stock her products. She began to export her sleeves. All of this happened in less than five years. She began small, and used her profits to finance her expansion, resulting in low financial risk to her. This is just one example; many others exist.

Another area to consider is to do a job better than it is already being done. One successful small business started when a doctor's receptionist overheard two of the patients complaining about their hired house-cleaners. The receptionist said, 'Hire me. I'll do a better job.' One of the two patients did hire her and, true to her word, the receptionist did a better job. The ex-receptionist now has a team of house-cleaners. Her success has been based on delivering top value for money.

Reliability is an increasingly rare and much appreciated attribute these days and it could be the unique quality that sets your business apart from the rest. When young Aron Ritchie knocked on the door of a friend of mine and asked if he could mow her lawns, she came back with question: What did he have to offer that was special? Her ears pricked up when he guaranteed that he would always turn up (subject to weather, of course), or if he couldn't, he'd ring her. He got the job. Five years later he is still mowing my friend's lawn (and those of many of her friends) and they call him Mr Reliable. Aron never advertises ... he's too busy keeping up with the demands of word-of-mouth customers who, like my friend, value his reliability as much as his lawnmowing skills.

3. Use existing skills or gain new expertise

If you can provide a unique service or product using your existing skills or expertise, you are off to a good start. You will often feel more comfortable, at least initially, supplying goods and services you are familiar with, or which are a logical extension of your existing skills and talents. In many cases skills and knowledge gained in one industry might readily be transferred to another (eg. selling skills gained in sales and marketing could help close a gardening deal; bookkeeping ability is required in every business).

If you aim to go into business in an unfamiliar activity, then educate yourself in that area before doing anything else. This might necessitate formal study, perhaps while still working in another career; or informal study (e.g. buying books and trade magazines and reading them at home), It would be good experience to work for someone else in a similar business, perhaps full time, or part-time on weekends or at night, to gain experience before branching out on your own.

The important thing is to determine what skills and knowledge you will need and to make sure you obtain them. This also requires some prior research.

Your business knowledge will also play a huge part in your success or failure. Many people who are true experts in their field have failed because they lacked business know-how. You must be able to cost a job accurately and provide value for money. One landscape company foreman felt cheated because he was the person who saw that the job was completed and managed well, yet the profits went to the company owner. He believed that the 'business' side would be easy, so he went to work for himself. What he didn't realise was that, while he was an excellent project manager, he was not very good at costing jobs and dealing with customers. Fortunately for him, he was able to return to his previous job.

4. Get your advertising right

Experimentation: that is the key. Do not spend a lot of money until you have properly worked out what does and does not work for you. Try small

Industry trade shows provide opportunities to speak to people in the industry and to acquire business contacts.

advertisements in a range of publications, perhaps classifieds at first. Try different types of advertisements. I have advertised in more than 200 different publications, of which only around 20% have been worthwhile. Try press releases. Send them to magazines, newspapers and radio stations. Record where your *responses* come from and where your *firm business* comes from (e.g. one publication might yield 30 responses and none of them result in business, while another might only provide five responses, but two of these respondents do business with you).

Talk to others in the industry. Find out what advertising strategies have and have not been successful for them. Join an industry group to make contacts. Many business people will share their information, allowing you to learn from the mistakes of others.

5. Get your prices right
Many businesses go broke because they charge too little. Henry Ford may have become a billionaire by selling a large number of cars at very cheap prices but, more often than not, people are just as happy to pay a higher price if you give them quality and good service. Remember, small business is just that—small. If you are going to succeed with the low price/high turnover formula, you need to be operating on a large scale, usually with a high level of investment.

6. Get your costs right

All too often, small businesses pay more than they need to for materials and equipment. If you take your time before starting to thoroughly check out suppliers, and learn to negotiate about prices, you can establish much lower costs for your business before you begin. Remember, every dollar extra you pay in costs is a dollar less in your pocket.

7. Be prepared for a modest start

Usually the first few years of any small business will require long hours, perhaps a six- or seven-day week; and all this for perhaps a smaller return than you would get working in a normal 9 to 5 job. If you have money or other resources set aside, or supplementary income (e.g. your partner/spouse has a full time job) as a backup to cover you through this lean period, you will have a much greater chance of success.

It is important that you and your family consider the many sacrifices that come with starting up a small business, including less money to spend on entertainment, no time for travel or holidays, longer working hours, etc. If you do not have the full support and understanding of the family, then making the business work becomes doubly difficult.

8. Make the customer No. 1

A happy customer is the best asset a new business can have. You will not only get more follow-up business from existing customers, but they will be your best source of advertising, simply by word of mouth (see Aron's story in Point 2). There is truth in the saying 'One happy customer will tell one other person. One unhappy customer will tell ten others.'

9. Monitor your competition

Subscribe to any magazines or newspapers that report on the industry in which you are operating. Monitor advertisements in that industry. Keep a close eye on any other business offering similar services or products, and watch out for any new businesses that might offer competition. Join industry associations or mentor groups comprised of other small business people, especially those with gardening or landscaping knowledge, who can provide advice and support.

10. Diversify ASAP—but not too much

Initially you should not try to provide too many different types of goods or services, but once your business gets on its feet, look for other services or products that might complement what you are already doing. Demands change, that is a fact of life. If you do one thing only, you will find there will be times when your business will boom and other times when it will be slow. If you do several things, there is a good chance that when one thing slows, the others will still perform well.

Keep in mind, though, that you cannot be all things to all people. If you diversify, try to add a business or service that complements, but does not detract from, your core business. For instance, the addition of a restaurant service to an existing bed and breakfast could be a good diversification. It complements and could even increase the B&B business; likewise the addition of weed control services to a lawnmowing round.

11. Don't go overboard

There is a natural tendency for your sense of self importance to grow when you are the boss and, as that happens, there is an inclination to increase the size of your business beyond what is reasonable. Immodest employers tend to employ more people than are required, advertise more than is needed, and produce more than they can sell. Just because a business is bigger doesn't mean it is run better or is more profitable. In many cases well run smaller businesses can be very profitable, and enable you as the boss to keep good control (oversight) of the activities of the business.

Part of your long-term business plan should include what you want personally in the long run. Creating a large enterprise that is still growing when you are ready to retire can cause a real dilemma. Many people start up in small business because they want a more relaxed lifestyle. This can be achieved, as long as you recognise your own goals.

12. Take care of your staff

Good quality staff are the most valuable asset in any business. If you are loyal and have a generous and flexible attitude towards your staff, they will respond in kind.

13. Take care of yourself

You must be healthy to deal with the stresses associated with running a business and still be able to think clearly and operate efficiently. Healthy businessmen put in fewer hours and achieve far more than those who neglect their basic needs, such as exercise, diet, rest and recreation. Running your own business is not just about making money, it is also about taking control of your life. Ideally, your business should give you the financial rewards, job satisfaction and personal flexibility you desire. This may not happen initially, and in fact is unlikely early on in the life of a new business, but it should be a medium- to long-term aim of the business.

POTENTIAL PITFALLS

- **Advertising that you will do anything** (when you don't have the skill or the equipment to do many gardening jobs).

- **Underquoting when you first start your business.** It is best to work on an hourly rate, at least until you become familiar with what you are capable of getting done in a given time.

- **Neglecting to include overheads in a quote.** It costs you time and money to travel to a job, to give a quote in the first place, to supply tools, run an office, maintain equipment, etc. All of these costs have to be covered.

- **Wanting to get a job, no matter what.** There are plenty of people who think gardeners should be cheap labour; there are others who think cheap gardeners are not good gardeners. You should not be afraid to lose a job because you are too expensive. Someone else may hire you just because you're not cheap.

- **Liquidity problems.** Some types of garden service jobs require you to have a certain amount of cash in hand. If you are not paid for a landscape job until weeks or months after doing the work, you need to have sufficient money available to carry you for that period. If your work is seasonal, you need to save enough in the good times to keep you going in the bad times.

- **Not being specific about what is included in a quote.** Clients may expect free garden maintenance after a landscape job. Some people expect free removal of rubbish after a pruning job. Others expect you to come back and spray again free of charge if your first pest or weed spraying doesn't work. Some clients expect the roots to be removed as well as the top of a tree when you quote on tree removal, or for all of the wood to be cut up into short blocks suitable for firewood. Clearly state *everything* that is to be included on the job and don't feel pressured to do more than you contracted for.

- **Make sure the client understands what you will or won't do!**

Legal Requirements

In Australia legal requirements that must be met by different businesses vary from state to state and indeed from local council to local council, not to mention the requirements of water, gas and electricity authorities; no doubt the same variance occurs in other countries, too. It is most important that all requirements be checked out. In some instances nurseries or landscape contractors must be registered with the government, or perhaps be involved in an industry accreditation scheme.

Every business has certain obligations to keep financial records for taxation purposes. Staff must be employed in accordance with other regulations. In some situations, workplaces must be registered or approved by government authorities. Businesses must be structured in a way that complies with legal requirements, and you must understand, decide upon and set up an appropriate structure if you are to minimise legal liability for anything that happens in your business.

Most state governments have departments that provide advice to small businesses about what rules, regulations, etc. are relevant to their business. It is important that you find out what these are. Trade or industry organisations (e.g. Landscape Industry Associations) are also valuable sources of information. Licensing may be required for the tasks you plan to perform. Check with your local government authorities. You will find some useful contacts in the Appendix, together with their address and phone numbers.

Nursery trade shows and individual nurseries are sources for plants and growing advice.

Professional advice

As a business person, you are a professional. Respect the fact that, to be successful, you will need assistance from other professionals. The advice of a good lawyer and a good accountant can be invaluable. Even advice from more experienced professional people within your industry may benefit your business—for example, getting the advice of professional irrigation consultants or horticulturists instead of trying to bluff your way through a job. You do not always have to follow their advice, but being better informed will help you to make sound decisions.

TWO WAYS TO BEGIN IN BUSINESS

There are two common ways to get into your own business: one is to start your own, and the other is to buy an existing business.

Before you start

As well as ascertaining the possibilities of the market, it is important to find out as much as possible about your own personal and financial potential as well as the skills you now possess and/or intend to acquire. Try the following checklist:

1. Why do you want your own business? '...because I hate my current boss' isn't a good enough reason. Is it because you prefer to be your own boss? Because you think you can make more money working for yourself? Because you want more flexibility in your working hours? Because you have a great idea for a service or particular goods? You need to be really clear about your own motivations for running your own business.

2. Are you the type of person to tackle a business? Can you handle pressure, people, hard work, etc? Could you cope with the needs of an expanding business?

3. Do you understand the business you have in mind? Don't go in blind. Joe Bloggs might be making millions—you might not!

4. What are your chances of success? Study the market and make some assessments. Do you have the relevant skills and/or knowledge, or can you easily get them?

5. Can you afford to start? Have you the capital, and some money in reserve for living expenses until the business gets going? Do you have a fall-back option if the business does not prosper or takes longer than expected to get on its feet (e.g. your partner or spouse has an income)?

The priority is to find out as much as possible about yourself as well as any potential business.

Seeking advice

No one is an expert in every facet of running a business. It can often save you a great deal of time, effort, money (and grief) to consult experts in a particular field. These include lawyers, accountants, insurance brokers, government small business departments and local council staff. You should be able to claim as a tax deduction any fees you pay these experts. You may also want to talk to consultants in the field that you are entering.

A few hints
* Most of the major banks have leaflets/brochures on topics such as business planning, financing businesses, and franchising. It is worth talking to your local bank branch about these.
* The Australian Government Publishing Service, in association with the National Executive of Small Business Agencies (NESBA) and AusIndustry, has developed a series of excellent books relating to various aspects of small business. They are well worth looking at and can be obtained from the Australian Government Publishing Service, which has shops in many major cities in Australia.
* Most Australian State Governments have agencies that specialise in assisting small businesses For example, in Victoria 'Small Business Victoria' provides advice and a wide variety of publications relating to setting up and running a small enterprise.

Note
Legal requirements vary in different states and countries. Even if you do not use an accountant regularly it is advisable that you consult one when setting up a new business, to ensure that your financial and legal record keeping is established properly.

STARTING A NEW BUSINESS V BUYING ONE

Starting a new business

The market niche
This is best when competition is weak, non-existent or not keeping up with the growing market or customer demands/requirements. It can be good if customer loyalty is not a factor, or if you can bring customers with you. Keep in mind that once you approach a niche market, a larger competitor may decide to move into that market. Be prepared for competition, even if it doesn't exist in the early days.

Personal aspects
Starting a new business can be a greater challenge than buying an established

Looking at good gardens can inspire work with future landscape jobs.

operation, and thus more satisfying when you are successful. You can start when you are ready, or you can start part-time initially. You have the freedom to introduce your own ideas and style from the beginning. However, there is more worry and pressure, it requires certain skills and attitudes (see 'Before you start'), and it takes time to research, decide, organise and become competent.

Goodwill

You start with a fresh slate with potential customers; you do not have to pay the 'goodwill' premium of an existing business. It is hard, however, to predict volume and market patterns, and there is generally a greater risk of a new business failing because it lacks an initial customer base.

Location

You can choose your own site for your business in the best available area, or the area that best suits you (e.g. close to home). If you are going to have leased facilities you will have them for the full lease period. On the other hand, all the good sites may already be occupied, and choosing an alternative site may involve a bit of guessing. You might also have to upgrade any new premises to meet regulations, or your own requirements, or to provide the necessary decor or services for your customers.

Staff
When starting a new business you can start small, and hire people to fit your particular needs and style. When employing staff, consider what weaknesses you may have and try to select some people who have strengths in those areas.

Equipment and stock
You can select the most modern equipment, or choose fresh stock, but they take time to select, ship and install, and the costs are high. The risk may prove untenable.

Financing
You can start small, but many costs are commonly not foreseen. Suppliers may require cash on delivery (COD), financing may be hard to come by, and slow initial cash flow can make servicing debts difficult.

Buying an Established Business

The market niche
It is best when the business you are buying is one of the main players in a market dominated by several strong competitors; or when a business has unique advantages such as location, name or rights/licensing agreements. However, you must be prepared to meet or exceed the standards established by the vendor.

Personal aspects
It is difficult to make changes or stamp your own style on an existing business. If it is well established it has proved it can work, so pressure on you is often less, although not always, particularly if you have difficulty being accepted by the existing staff.

Goodwill
With an existing business you acquire a ready-made clientele and the risk is thus reduced. Volume and market patterns are known; you can have immediate sales, and can therefore more readily cover operating costs. The most important thing here is to be sure that the vendor has not misrepresented the viability of the enterprise. Advice from an accountant, and perhaps a survey on your part of existing customers of the business, could save you a lot of grief.

Location
The business may have a valuable and unique location; lease terms may be favourable, and state and municipal code requirements should already have

been met. It could be decorated and serviced for customer needs and be immediately useable. On the other hand, it might be in a bad location and locked into unfavourable lease terms. *Check these out thoroughly!*

Staff

Your newly acquired staff may be experienced, tested over time, and able to assist greatly in the transition of the business into your control. Conversely, they might be deadwood, or incompatible with you, or resistant to change.

Equipment and stock

The equipment (including tools) is probably in working order and ready to use, but you should thoroughly check its condition. Maintenance records should also be checked. There may be problems if equipment is in poor condition or obsolete—it might be hard to obtain finance for new equipment and/or sell the old equipment.

Stock will most likely be already assembled and suppliers known. It is important to check the type and condition of existing stock—if it is 'dead stock', you may have no more success in moving it than did the previous owner.

Financing

The vendor may assist in financing, or conventional lenders may back you. Suppliers may more readily give credit than if you were opening a new business because they would expect you to have immediate cash flow, but the asking price for the business may be unrealistically high, or beyond your means. Goodwill cost is generally included, and is usually hard to borrow for.

Buying into a franchise

There are many franchises in the garden care industry. Some specialise in lawn maintenance, some offer specialist services, and others diverge to offer a range of services.

There are advantages in a well run franchise business. Costs can be shared with other franchisees in many areas, including advertising, other promotions, product/service development, etc. There can also be an advantage in reduced costs through bulk purchasing of materials or equipment.

There are also disadvantages. You can lose some control over decisions in your business. You may be restricted to operating within a certain geographic area, or from offering different products or services when the opportunity arises. There is also scope for unethical operators to take advantage of their franchisees.

It is important to note that anyone considering franchising into garden care or landscaping should be trained in that particular field. Too often stories are heard of customers paying for poor workmanship by untrained people. The public have elected to vote with their wallets; there is a noticeable increase in the number of qualified people now being employed, and customers are benefiting from their qualifications and reputation.

Although may people have successfully worked a franchise, many others have lost a great deal of money in set-up fees and establishment costs. The risk of business failure is great due to the fact that many people who buy into a franchise have no business experience and do not undertake any form of business training. The key to success in a franchise is:

- Conduct research about the prospective franchise and the industry it will cater for.
- Do a small business course.
- Undertake training in the industry the franchise is involved in.
- Check with government consumer affairs departments to determine whether there have been any complaints about the franchise operation you are considering.
- Above all, talk with people who have operated franchises for the company you are considering dealing with. It is a good idea to look up franchisees of that company in the phone book or local paper.

WHAT RECORDS DO I NEED TO KEEP?

The very minimum of records to keep are:

1. Simple cash book
In this you record all your daily receipts and all daily expenditure. Each week or month this can be totalled up to keep a cumulative balance.

2. Cheque book
Record all details of the transaction: date, to whom payment is made, amount, what the payment is for.
It is also very wise to keep the butts up to date with your deposits. This ensures that you know the balance of money in your bank account and how much you have to work with.

3. Bank statements
This is not only a record for your bank, but it helps you keep track of all amounts credited to and debited from your account/s. Check off all your cheques to ensure they have been presented and that your account has been debited with the correct amounts. Adjust the balance for unpresented cheques.

4. Receipt book
This should show: who paid, how much they paid, what service they paid for, and the date they paid.

5. Debtors' unpaid invoices

6. Creditors' unpaid invoices
Without keeping track of items 5 and 6 you can, without realising it, be well over your head in debt ... or you may be losing money because clients have not paid their bills.

7. Balance sheet
Records all incomings and outgoings at one point in time. This allows you to see the overall financial position of your business—it is the big picture. It will also be necessary for tax purposes.

8. Customer profiles
These should include as much detail as possible about your customers, but at a minimum should include contact addresses, phone and fax numbers and the person/s you deal with.

PROMOTING A NEW BUSINESS

When you commence business you must promote yourself and the services you are going to offer. This can be done in a variety of ways, including:

1. Local newspaper advertising
2. Major daily newspaper advertising
3. Magazine advertising
4. Letterbox drops
5. Direct mail promotions
6. Telephone books (i.e. Yellow Pages)
7. The Internet
8. Other (e.g. press releases, product launches, etc.)

Local newspaper advertising
The trade directory is usually the most successful place. Prepare a sample design of an advertisement, then have a few friends and relatives look at it to see what they think. What sort of information did it convey to them? Did it grab their attention? You might get the newspaper to design your ad for you. This type of ad works well for small businesses servicing home gardens (ie. lawnmowing, landscaping, pruning, rubbish removal, etc). Often a small ad works as well as a big one, and it will be a lot cheaper to run. Several tiny classified advertisements will frequently get better results than you might get from one larger ad that costs the same amount of money for one insertion.

Major daily newspaper advertising
Classifieds in Saturday papers often give best value for money. Larger display

ads work well for some services at certain times of the year. But be careful: they can be expensive, and unless you get a lot of business from them, they are best avoided. They are better suited to advertising for larger scale work (ie. landscaping rather than weeding). Again, small ads often give the best value for each advertising dollar.

BEWARE OF LONG-TERM CONTRACTS!

When you first take out an advertisement in a newspaper or magazine be wary about being locked into long-term contracts. It may be cheaper per advertisement to book your ad in multiple issues (e.g. once a month for 12 months), but if the ad is not working after the first few months you may have wasted a lot of money. Usually it is best to trial your advertisement for a month or two to see what sort of response you get, then decide if you want more regular bookings.

Magazine advertising
Similar to daily newspapers. In Australia, *Your Garden* and *Gardening Australia* magazines are two of the best. If you don't get a response there, you are unlikely to get a reaction in other magazines.

Letterbox drops
Usually you will get between 1 and 5 responses for every few hundred letterboxes you drop a leaflet into ... depending on how good the leaflet is and how well you have chosen the area. For example, a leaflet on pruning dropped in summer in a new housing estate will not get any response; in winter, in an old-established, wealthy area it will likely bring in some work. Likewise, a leaflet for new garden landscaping services will most likely do better in a new estate than in an old-established one.

Direct mail
Letters or leaflets can be sent to real estate agents, shopping centre managers, council parks departments and anyone else you think might employ people to do gardening work. Often you will get the best response by following these mail-outs with a phone call. Sometimes mail-outs work, sometimes they are a dead loss.

Telephone book
Many people find the Yellow Pages to be the best advertising of all. Some don't! Overall it is probably one of your better chances. Be careful when you first start advertising that you aren't persuaded to take out expensive display ads. It is best to test the waters at first with a smaller advertisement, to see what sort of response you get. As your business becomes better established you might then progress to a larger ad.

Exhibitions and shows

I have known landscapers and garden care companies to mount a display once each year at a garden show and get enough business from that effort to keep them employed for six months. I have known others to work for a week at a garden show and get no work from it at all.

Home shows and various types of industry exhibitions can be equally profitable (or unprofitable). This method of advertising works well if you exhibit the right product or service at the right time, in the right way and at the right show. You must get these variables right, and generally you must make a considerable and often costly investment; so do not exhibit at a show without giving it a lot of forethought.

The Internet

The Internet was of little significance to gardeners or landscapers in the past, but that situation is changing very rapidly. A growing number of people are connected to and using the Internet for all sorts of information. More and more landscapers, nurserymen and gardeners are using the net to promote their businesses. Even if you do not consider the Internet when you start, you should consider it as a serious promotional tool in the future. It can also be a valuable research tool.

Other methods

There are many other ways of getting work. Leaflets and business cards can be put on public notice boards or in shop windows; you can advertise in community directories or on calendars; you can take a series of radio or theatre ads … these methods sometimes work, but are very often no good at all. Read the tenders section in the Saturday newspaper classifieds. Various organisations call for people to give a quote to do a job. Often different types of gardening work are advertised. Offering unpaid work for community charities can also lead to paid business.

UNDERSTANDING CONTRACT LAW

Whenever you take on a job, large or small, you are entering into a legal contract. Under contract law, *a contract does not need to be written down*—but doing so can make things simpler. A contract is made whenever one party offers something (e.g. to design a garden for a certain amount of money) and another party (the client) accepts the offer.

In most cases, there is no problem—the contractor does what is expected, and the client pays what is expected—but if either one does not do what is expected by the other, there is a dispute. If the agreement has been written down, the parties can look at the written contract and the dispute can usually be easily settled. If things are not written down, it may need to go to court.

Often the best way to sort out any potential problems is to explain your business activities to a lawyer and have them make recommendations as to what should be included in any contracts you might undertake.

Avoiding disputes

The best way to avoid disputes is to try to foresee anything that might go wrong and include these possible eventualities within a contract, to be signed by both parties before any work is started.

For example, if you are a lawnmowing contractor you need to develop a standard quotation form. This form should state what you will do. It may say things such as:

- Lawn clippings are taken away (or are put in the compost heap).
- Edges are trimmed with a whipper snipper.
- Lawns are mown at a height of 2.5 cm.
- The lawn is to be mown every 1 to 3 weeks, the frequency being in accordance with growth rates but totally at the discretion of the contractor.
- Any other work such as raking the surface, treating damaged patches, etc. is to be quoted as extra tasks.
- Payment is to be made immediately upon completion of each mowing. If payment is delayed, a 5% additional cost per week will be incurred.
- The contract is to last for six months and then be reviewed.

Generally a larger job will involve a more complex contract. Large landscape contracts can involve a package of documents including several plans, written specifications for materials, and a contract of several pages specifying all terms, conditions and contingencies. In such situations, legal advice before quoting is essential.

2
What Services Could You Offer?

In many two-income households time for domestic tasks is limited, which is why house cleaning, child care and gardening services are boom industries today. The services you could consider providing include:

Lawn mowing   Normally done on a weekly or fortnightly basis in the active growing seasons, less often in winter.
May include trimming edges on each cut, on every second or third cut, or not at all.
May be 'quality cut' service for top quality lawns, using top quality cylinder mowers.
May be basic cutting service using standard rotary type mower.
The service may or may not include removal of lawn clippings from the site.

Pruning   May be provided as part of a routine maintenance contract which you attend to every week, fortnight or month.
Is also done as a once-off, or once-a-year job, e.g. roses and deciduous fruit trees in winter.

Tree lopping   Involves removal of unwanted or dangerous branches from trees—normally a one-off job.
Special equipment and skill are needed to do this safely and properly.
Insurance costs are generally quite high.

Tree surgery   A highly specialised area of tree work requiring more skill and experience than tree lopping. Strictly for arboriculturists.

Weeding   Could be a one-off job, but is more commonly part of a regular maintenance contract.
May involve chemical weed control (spraying) or other methods (hand weeding).

Garden maintenance may require care of the lawn and other garden plants, and general cleaning.

Seasonal replanting of seedlings may be required by some older property owners who have lost some of their agility.

Pest control Normally involves identification and spraying to control pests and diseases, but may also involve other control methods.

Lawn renovation Involves repairing and improving an existing lawn. Could include such things as topdressing, weed control, thatch removal, aerating, feeding and watering.

General garden maintenance Usually encompasses work on a weekly or fortnightly basis for a set number of hours, to do some or all of the jobs needed to care for the garden (i.e. feeding, watering, weeding, lawn mowing, pest control, pruning, etc.).

Rubbish removal Often included in a gardening job, and often expected! You should clearly indicate to customers whether you do or do not remove rubbish.

Garden renovation Normally a one-off job involving weeding, pruning, spraying, replacing dead plants, additional planting, lawn renovation and perhaps some minor landscaping.

Landscaping Usually a more extensive task than other garden services. Involves such things as earthworks, rock work, drainage, lawn construction, paving, installation of watering systems, planting, etc.

Landscape design May offer design advice or a full landscape plan. Often, but not always, attached to a nursery or landscaping business.

Irrigation design and installation A service used by home owners, factories, estate developers, councils, etc. The move to water efficiency has seen an increase in irrigation system sales and installation in recent years.

Indoor plant care Involves installation and maintenance of plants in offices, buildings and display areas.
Calls for routine maintenance once a week in most situations.
Some fields listed above will require registration in appropriate associations. It would be in your interest to achieve acceptance into these associations as they can promote business. In any case, it is strongly recommended that before offering a plant-related service to the public, you should receive training in that particular field.

OTHER OPTIONS

The options suggested above are traditional services that comprise the vast bulk of activities in garden and landscape businesses. They are less risky than new, niche, or trendy areas, and probably offer a greater opportunity for a secure income for most people. However, there are other options, and if you are able to be innovative you may do well to develop a different type of service in a new or niche area.

Niche markets

The world is a diverse place and there are always small groups of people who will respond to unique services and products that are not generally offered. To be successful, you need to develop something different at the right time and in the right place and to establish your business before any serious competition develops. Some examples are:

Garden consultancy
This business will require formal qualifications and experience. The tasks involved may cover pest and disease identification and control, advice on garden design and choice of fruit and vegetable, fung shui, etc. It may be possible to charge more, as it would be a professional service. You can provide written reports and advice. This business may link up with other businesses that do landscape construction or other tasks if your consultancy business is not set up for it.

Courtyard designing
This business would deal specifically with small-lot properties such as town houses, etc. A high degree of skill would be expected, with an eye for detail and perfection. It is a service that would be best directed towards inner city dwellers.

Hydroponic landscaping
This specialist could design and install a garden area that is completely hydroponic. The client would have a relatively hassle-free garden that looks good and provides fruits, herbs and vegetables for the table. Routine maintenance, perhaps once a month, might be offered as an optional extra service.

Themed landscaping
Japanese, Malaysian, Santa Fe, Rainforest, Native, etc. are all theme gardens that a business could specialise in designing and constructing.

Topiary or bonsai maintenance
This business could provide routine maintenance for bonsai or topiary plants, potting up, feeding, and pruning or training. Such a service would only succeed in places where there are affluent clients with topiary or bonsai collections.

Holiday garden care

This business could offer to take care of gardens when the owners go on holiday. People who might not normally employ a gardener could be attracted to such a service. It could take time to develop a business like this, and the work might be seasonal (e.g. long hours in summer and short working weeks in winter).

Water management

This business might specialise in helping a gardener reduce water consumption by better garden management. The service could involve such things as installing irrigation, mulching a garden, installing deep watering pipes for large trees, changing plant varieties, or redesign of gardens for better water conservation.

Plant finder service

This business may source out various nurseries for clients who are after specific plant species (usually the rare and unique). Instead of the client running around, you may be hired to do the searching and collecting the plants. Plants may range from a small 140 mm pot to a 4-metre trees, individually or in large numbers. The services of a plant finder could be used by other nurseries, councils, landscape companies and home gardeners.

Complementary fringe services

There are various other services that are not strictly 'gardening', but are often provided as an extra service. If appropriate, you might consider offering the following extra 'value-added' services along with the business you develop.

• **Swimming pool maintenance.** This can comprise vacuuming, testing water, adding chemicals if needed, and cleaning the pool filter.
• **Building maintenance.** This might involve simple things such as painting, removing/treating rust on metal surfaces, oiling squeaking hinges, repairing any damage to walls or doors, etc.
• **Cleaning gutters and/or windows.** Uncluttered gutters may be especially appreciated by home-owners in a high-risk area for bushfires.
• **Firewood supply.** Gardeners sometimes have the opportunity to remove firewood from one property, store and dry it, and then sell it to another client as firewood.

CONSIDERING THE OPTIONS

When you start anything new, try to avoid doing too much too soon. Gardening is no different from anything else. Some areas of gardening work are relatively easy to do—they do not require a lot of skill or capital outlay in order to do a reasonable job. Other gardening services are more involved, and careful consideration and detailed planning should be carried out before entering business in those spheres. Table 2.1 will give you a quick reference when considering what services you might offer in your gardening business.

ASPECTS TO CONSIDER BEFORE OPENING A GARDEN BUSINESS				
BUSINESS	RISK	SEASON	SKILL	OVERHEADS
Lawnmowing	LR	AYS	LS	LO-MO
Pruning	MR	Wint	MS	MO-HO
Tree lopping	R	AY	MS	MO-HO
Tree surgery	HR	AY	HS	HO
Weeding	MR	AY & Sp	MS	LO
Pest control	R	Sp, Sum, Aut	MS-HS	MO
Weed spraying	MR	AY & Sp	MS	MO
Lawn renovation	R	Sp & Aut	HS	MO-HO
General garden maint.	LR	AY	LS-MS	LO
Rubbish removal	LR	AY	LS	MO
Garden renovation	R	AY & Sp	MS-HS	MO-HO
Landscaping	HR	Sp, Sum, Aut	HS	HO
Irrigation design & install.	HR	AY	MS-HS	MO-HO
Interior plant service	R	AYS	LS	MO

KEY

Risk

LR Low risk

MR Medium—can be considered by someone new to the industry.

R Risky unless you prepare yourself properly to offer this service.

HR High risk—an area where business failures are common, particularly if you are not properly prepared.

Season

Sp Spring

Sum Summer

Aut Autumn

Wint Winter

AY All year

AYS All year—seasonal peaks

Skill

LS Low skill level required

MS Medium skill required

HS High skill required

Overheads

(hidden costs, insurance, equipment, etc.)

LO Low level overheads

MO Medium level overheads

HO High overheads

WHAT DO YOU NEED TO START?

The following information lists only the minimum or basic requirements for each activity. As finances permit, more comprehensive or specialised equipment and tools might be obtained.

Note: Appropriate safety equipment, in good condition, should be used for all activities and should be included when assessing basic requirements. This might include safety glasses, boots and gloves; protective clothing such as spray suits or chain saw pants; full face masks and/or respirators for spraying, and safety harnesses if climbing trees.

Duties involved in each of the following services are detailed in Chapter 4, 'Garden Maintenance Services'; advice on the maintenance of tools and equipment is given in Chapter 5, 'Gardening and Landscaping Tools'.

LAWNMOWING

Equipment A reliable lawn-mower (preferably 2 or 3 mowers). At least one mower have a grass catcher.

For larger lawns, a ride-on mower may be required.

Lawn edging tools.

A car with trailer, station wagon or utility.

A leaf rake.

An air blower or a yard broom.

Contract Normally a handshake contract (nothing legal). Payment is normally made at the end of each day.

Payment may be based on a fixed quote or on an hourly rate.

Comments There are correct and incorrect ways to mow grass. A knowledgeable person will not only do a better job, but will do it quicker, although anyone with a little common sense and willingness to work can do this job.

LARGE MOWING JOBS (ACREAGE, SPORTS FIELDS, ETC.)

Equipment Slashers, gang mowers, etc. are required to save time in mowing.

Quality of cut grass will be dependent on equipment used and the condition of the area to be mowed (e.g. even or uneven, clean or lots of debris).

General hand tools for machinery maintenance and one-off jobs.

Contract Often done under contract—sometimes a handshake deal.

Payment usually at the conclusion of the job.

For large estates, councils or government authorities it may be on monthly accounts.

A fixed rate for the property is the most usual method for regular customers, hourly rates for new customers.

Comments Provided equipment is good, little technical knowledge is required

Acreage will require regular slashing—a service much in demand. Notice how paths can be achieved by slashing a strip.

Tree pruning and surgery are best done by qualified and licensed arboriculturists. Either become trained in that field or have contacts you can pass on to your customer.

to carry out these jobs. Care may be needed near established plants, structures, water features and steep slopes. Insurance costs can be fairly high.

PRUNING

Equipment Several good pairs of secateurs and a good pruning saw.

Short-handled loppers and high pruners (for small high branches)

A free-standing step-ladder.

Transport capable of carrying a ladder (a roof rack may be needed)

Contract As for lawnmowing.

Comments Most pruning work is during the winter months. Many gardeners spend winter pruning and the rest of the year doing other jobs such as landscaping or lawn repair, etc.

Pruning work is mainly on roses and fruit trees. It takes some skill to prune these plants, though it is possible to get a basic ability with a few days' practice and a little study. It can take years, however, to become an expert at pruning.

TREE LOPPING

This is not the same as tree surgery! Tree lopping involves removing trees or parts of trees that grow where your client does not want them to grow. Tree surgery involves operating on the tree to try to improve its health or wellbeing.

Equipment An extension ladder.

Good secateurs.

A step ladder.

A variety of ropes (jute rather than nylon).

2 chain saws (light & heavyweight & spare parts).

2 bow saws (small & large, & spare blades).

Other items such as a mulcher, climbing harness, winches, etc. can be useful and may be considered.

Contracts As for lawnmowing.

Comments This can be dangerous for both the gardener and for the client's property if you don't do things properly. You can fall, branches can fall on you, branches can fall on buildings, washing lines, power lines and fences. Ropes can be used to lower branches slowly and avoid damage. If you cut in the right place you can determine how and where a branch will fall. A lot of people who offer this service do not have the appropriate skill or knowledge to do a proper job. Accidents do occur. They might not always damage property or person, but they can damage your reputation. Adequate Public Liability insurance is vital in this field.

TREE SURGERY

Equipment All the requirements for tree lopping plus a winch, harness and extra ropes.

Wood chisels and trenching tool for trimming bark damage and cleaning out decay from cavities.

Power drill and bits and suitable hand tools (e.g. hammer, spanners, pliers) for cabling and bolting work.

Contract Normally charges are higher than for lopping.

A written quote is usually given for a job rather than working at an hourly rate.

Comments Tree surgery techniques are highly skilled procedures requiring knowledge and resources beyond someone commencing a new business. You are advised to study and read and have suitable work experience with an established tree surgeon before offering these services.

Insurance requirements should be investigated and liabilities established clearly before starting a job.

HAND WEEDING

Equipment Very little is needed for hand weeding—perhaps some gardening gloves, a good hoe and maybe a small hand trowel or fork.

For larger areas and difficult weeds a larger digging fork may be required.

Contract As for lawnmowing.

Comments Requires minimal skill, but does involve a lot of bending and as such is not recommended if you have a bad back.

You need to be able to tell the difference between a weed and a cherished garden plant.

PEST CONTROL

Equipment Good sprayer (if you plan on a lot of this work, you should have several types of sprayers—a 15-litre unit for small or medium jobs, perhaps a larger motorised unit for larger jobs. (See Chapter 5, Table 5.1 for a comparison of sprayers).

Measuring jars/jugs and containers for mixing chemicals.

Rubber gloves.

If using very poisonous chemicals, you require protective clothing, including head gear—hood, full face mask and respirator.

Contract Terms should be stated clearly on a standard contract, particularly with respect to safety and danger aspects.

Normally a fixed price contract.

Comments Insurance and liabilities should be established before commencing a job.

It is possible to do very well from spraying alone, and danger is minimal if safety precautions are followed. Some chemicals are extremely dangerous, though, and should be avoided wherever possible.

Chemical Application Licences are usually required—contact your local Department of Agriculture for information.

Medium to high skill levels (e.g. pest and product knowledge) are required.

A good knowledge of plants is important for correct diagnosing and recommendations.

WEED SPRAYING

Equipment As for pest control.

Contract As for pest control.

Comments Weedicides are generally safer to people than are insecticides.

Improper spraying can kill other 'wanted' plants. This may lead to action against the person who did the spraying.

See comments for pest control (these may apply)

LAWN RENOVATION

Equipment Solid, quality rake (rakes can break easily!)

Aerator fork, spade and shovel.

Wheelbarrow

Utility vehicle, truck or car and trailer.

Other equipment (i.e. level lawn rake, rotary hoe, mechanised renovation equipment).may be needed at times but is not essential as it can be hired as required.

Contract Normally fixed quote.

Payment either on completion or 30 day account.

Comments This type of business has been very successful overseas, but as yet is not a major part of the garden service industry in Australia. Many gardeners and landscapers do a certain amount of lawn renovation each year as part of their overall business.

GENERAL GARDEN MAINTENANCE

Normally involves weeding, lawn mowing, pruning, watering, fertilising, pruning and any other routine maintenance work.

Equipment Often equipment is supplied by the property owner.

Some jobs require the gardener to supply equipment (maybe only a lawn-mower), others require all necessary equipment to be supplied.

Private homes are more likely to supply equipment.

Contract   Usually a routine weekly or fortnightly job; payment is made at the end of each work session.

Public maintenance jobs, for government, factories, shopping centres, etc, usually work on a term contract. Payment is made on a monthly account.

Comments   Public maintenance contracts can provide good bread-and-butter money, but they will rarely make you rich. Don't overcommit yourself to contracts. Remember that you have to wait for payment on these jobs, and sometimes the bureaucrats can keep you waiting for 3–4 months. Make sure you have enough in the bank to keep you going while you wait.

RUBBISH REMOVAL

Equipment   A truck, utility or car with large trailer. If you are going to offer a casual removal service you can make do without a truck; for regular rubbish removal, though, a truck is the only efficient way. Ropes and tarpaulins.

Contract   Sometimes included in the cost of a general maintenance contract, pruning or landscape job. Sometimes charged as a separate job.

Comments   It may be worthwhile finding a rubbish removal contractor whom you can recommend to clients, rather than doing this work yourself. Rubbish removal can take quite a lot of time ... many tips will not accept garden rubbish; many will not accept rubbish from people who are not residents of that municipality. You may need to take the rubbish some distance to get rid of it. Most dumps will charge a fee for commercial use.

GARDEN RENOVATION

Equipment   Quality rake, shovel, spade, fork, crow bar, secateurs, pruning saw and wheelbarrow.

Car with trailer, utility or truck.

Contract   Normally a fixed-price contract.

Deposit of 10–30% before starting, balance on completion.

Comments   Generally small landscape jobs or garden renovations are the best place for an aspiring landscaper to start. Usually a job is not worth much more than $500. Payment is normally forthcoming without problems. Linking in with a garden designer may lead to being nominated as the preferred garden renovator.

LANDSCAPE CONTRACTING

Equipment   A variety of hand tools, including hammers, spanners, chisels, levels, string line, wheelbarrow and crow bar.

Power tools including saw (and suitable blades) and drill (and suitable bits).

Chainsaw (perhaps).

As for garden renovation, plus a rotary hoe and/or a small tractor/cat or similar machine (you can either own or hire machinery, but it is needed).

Contract Normally a fixed-price contract.

Deposit of 10–30% before starting.

Progress payment and balance on completion, or within an agreed time after completion.

Comments Maintenance of the landscape for 2 weeks to 3 months after completion is normally expected, as is removal of debris.

Landscapers experience a relatively high number of problems associated with people not paying, or bringing action against them to reclaim payment after completion of a job. These problems are normally associated with the client having different expectations about the job from what they see after completion. A landscaper can only start the process of growth of a garden; the client often expects the finished product on or soon after completion ... they are not prepared to wait for five years for the garden to grow. Even though you may have explained this, the client might just not understand.

Some states have licensing schemes for landscape contractors. Be sure to check what requirements there are in your state before setting up as a landscaper.

Associations exist in most states and countries for those set up as landscapers.

• *Be careful with landscaping!*
It is an area that has a lot of potential pitfalls and there is also a great deal of competition. This is not the type of business to commence without first preparing properly and obtaining at least some basic training and on-the-job experience. An advantage is to have a qualification and training in the field, with necessary licensing to carrying out particular types of jobs such as irrigation, fencing, non-attached buildings, pavers, etc.

Specialist niche areas for landscape construction
A landscape contractor might choose to start out by specialising in one or two areas, taking advantage of the things that s/he knows most about. Table 2.2 lists some options.

TABLE 2.2. NICHE AREAS FOR LANDSCAPE CONSTRUCTION

Paving	Fencing	Rockery construction
Bricklaying	Stone walls	Irrigation
Asphalt	Concreting	Formal gardens
Lawns	Earthworks	Cottage gardens
Herb gardens	Water gardens	Timber Structures
Bush gardens	Permaculture gardens	(e.g. pergolas, gazebos, etc)

IRRIGATION DESIGN AND INSTALLATION

Equipment Post hole digger, spade, shovel, metal rake, hand spanners, wheelbarrow, etc. Hiring of equipment such as trench diggers may be required at commencement of job.

Contract Normally a fixed-price contract.

Similar to landscape contracting.

Comments Training in irrigation equipment, products and design will be essential.

The digging of holes should only be done after verification of location of existing pipes and underground services.

In cases where soil is to be dug up, the client should be informed of potential soil disturbance and assured that it will be cleaned up.

Knowledge of plant requirements for irrigation is beneficial.

Excessive excavation may damage plant roots—be careful, and/or offer a guarantee if plants die.

It will be necessary to return to the job at a later date to ensure all is working as it should and to check that no sprinklers have been damaged, lost or removed.

INTERIOR PLANT SERVICE

Equipment Secateurs, watering can, misters, wipe cloth.

Staff usually carry a bucket or similar carrying mild insecticide, fertiliser, white oil, twist ties and other miscellaneous items that may be of use.

Vehicle to get from site to site, possibly a larger vehicle for plant installations and removals.

Contract Fixed price based on hours at each site and proximity to other clients.

Delicate plants which require more maintenance will require a higher fee.

Usually set for 12 month period.

Comments The high demand in travelling as part of the job by staff, and the wear and tear on vehicles, may result in high turnover of staff.

Job can be tedious, so it is important to keep the minds of staff active with training, promotions or other techniques.

Staff should be trained in fostering customer relations, as well as in plant diagnosing techniques and general plant care.

Low light and airconditioned buildings will deteriorate plants fast. It may be a good idea to establish a nursery for the growing on and rejuvenation of plants.

Associations now exist in many countries for those in this industry.

LANDSCAPE DESIGN

Equipment Basic survey equipment (e.g. a tape measure, north/south compass, and perhaps a dumpy level) for surveying the site.

Basic draughting equipment (e.g. black pens, ruler, French curves, templates for drawing different sized circles, compass, drawing table or a very smooth-topped desk—avoid a desk with any dints at all).

Contract Sometimes a fixed price, sometimes an hourly rate is charged, with an estimate of expected cost range being given first.

Comments Landscape design is a more skilled task than many other landscaping tasks and, as such, the hourly rate charged can easily

Designing, creating and installing original work will be remembered by clients and all visitors who see it. This is an example of work created by Melbourne sculptor, William Ricketts.

be double what might be charged for landscape contracting.

There can be legal implications if you make very bad decisions that impact upon the future landscape (e.g. choosing a tree that causes structural damage to a swimming pool, pipes or paving). It is best to be conservative with such choices unless you are particularly experienced and skilled.

Overheads can be relatively low. The biggest costs to set up this type of business are:

a. the cost of learning how to draw good landscape plans;

b. advertising/marketing costs.

Specialist areas for a landscape design business

A new landscape designer might offer either a general design service, or a specialist service concentrating on one type of landscape. Table 2.3 lists some options.

TABLE 2.3. DESIGN OPTIONS FOR THE LANDSCAPE DESIGNER

• Native gardens	• Dry or water-efficient gardens	• Large gardens
• Tropical gardens	• Vegetables and fruit	• Rainforest gardens
• Formal gardens	• Rose gardens	• Permaculture gardens
• Cottage gardens	• Outdoor living areas	• Japanese gardens
• Courtyards	• Herb gardens	• Children's playgrounds

FINDING MATERIALS

Materials such as plants, soil, timber and stone can comprise a large proportion of the costs involved in developing and maintaining any garden. Profitability and quality of service are both heavily dependent upon getting the right materials at the right price. Your suppliers might include:

Plant nurseries

Plants may be obtained from wholesale nurseries or one-stop landscape suppliers. Wholesale nurseries produce their own plants but can sell at a relatively cheap price; they can supply very large numbers of plants but may only produce a selected variety of plants species. The nursery will usually compile the plants for you to pick up. To get a large variety of plants you may need to go to a number of wholesale nurseries.

One-stop landscape suppliers usually stock soils, gravels, mulches and plants (either at wholesale or retail prices).

Wholesale redistribution centres are locations where a number of different wholesale nursery companies display their products. Landscapers can select what they want at their own leisure, or you may get the plants compiled for you at a fee. These places offer a great variety of plant species in a large range of pot sizes and prices.

Buying plants from retail nurseries is very expensive, unless you can organise a deal to buy at a discount for large orders. In some situations, it may be necessary to buy from these retail sources, such as when you require a specific rare or exotic plant and no wholesale nursery stocks it.

Sand, soil and screenings yards

These are local suppliers who buy bulk quantities of materials from quarries and other suppliers. They then resell smaller quantities at a higher price. It is appropriate to deal with these suppliers either because you require only small quantities of materials, or for convenience (i.e. you can get what you need relatively quickly from a local supplier).

Bulk suppliers

Quarries supply **gravel, sand and stone** in bulk, usually by the truckload. You cannot buy less than a truckload (possibly 8, 12 or more cubic metres).

• **Fill** is a product used in many landscapes where large volumes of soil are needed to increase the ground levels or alter the contours. Purchasing poor grade fill will affect plant growth and may cause secondary problems such as flooding areas and importing pests and diseases. Although fill is generally low-grade quality, ensure there is no plaster, concrete or other rubbish present. Remember that plant roots, especially from trees, will make their way down into the fill, so it should be conducive to plant root growth.

• **Woodshavings** are supplied in bulk from either timber mills or by contractors who have established deals to remove shavings from a mill.

• **Straw, sugar cane, manure and other organic materials** may be obtained in bulk quantities from some farms.

The cost of any bulk material will always increase greatly if it needs to be transported a long way. For this reason, if no other, the best bulk materials to use are always those that are produced locally. Look in the local Yellow Pages to find what quarries, mulch supplies, manure supplies, etc. are close to a job. These are often the best sources of material.

QUALITY CHECKING

Quality of plants and non-living materials (soils, rocks, etc) is very important to an industry that relies heavily on aesthetics. Even though the soil is covered by plants and mulch, its quality will influence the growth rate and health of plants. Plants need to be uniform when purchased and during their growth in order to satisfy the client at job conclusion and afterwards (especially if the landscape work comes with a warranty/guarantee). Pests or diseases observed on plants at purchase time should be an adequate reason for non-acceptance of the stock. This point should be either in the contract or understood between supplier and landscaper.

If you do not get good quality materials you can actually introduce problems to a garden.

- Gravel, soil or mulch can contain weeds. Look at what you buy before bringing it onto a site.
- If you see grass seeds in bales of straw, do not buy them.
- If you see weed plants or seeds in soil or gravel, don't use it.
- Only buy from reputable suppliers. Find out where materials came from, and avoid using sand from low-lying salt-contaminated coastal areas. Avoid materials which might introduce diseases or pests into a garden.

The test outlined in 'Naming the Soil' (Chapter 7) will help you to ascertain that you have received the type of soil you ordered.

- Some recycled timbers may rot, or may introduce termites. Others (e.g. railway sleepers impregnated with oils from years of lying under trains) may be very solid and unlikely to rot.
- Some organic materials contain toxic materials that can poison plant roots. Fresh pine bark, for instance, can deter garden plants from good growth but, if well composted before use, the same material can be an excellent soil additive or surface mulch. Materials containing toxins will generally have a sharp, strong smell (so smell soil or mulch before ordering it!).

In Australia and other countries, there are quality standards for garden soil mixes, just as there are for potting mixtures. Utilising soil mixes that meet these standards provides some level of assurance that plants will grow well—where such standards exist, it is strongly recommended that your soil purchases be guided accordingly. Landscaping with cheap grade soil will result in poor plant growth, which will reflect on the overall quality of the job.

EQUIPMENT AND TOOLS

Before you buy any tool or item of equipment you should decide whether you really need it. Often equipment is bought for the job on hand, used once, and never used again. At other times, the same piece of equipment is hired over and over, when it might have been more economical to buy your own.

Deciding to buy should be based on a genuine need for that piece of equipment, for such reasons as: significantly reducing workloads or the time involved in tasks; enabling you to expand the types of activities you undertake in the garden; safety; for improving the quality of your work. The need for the equipment should then be balanced against the cost, both initial and ongoing, and the operational requirements of that equipment. Is it really a worthwhile proposition? This must be decided on such factors as:

- Initial cost.
- Ongoing costs—this includes maintenance, parts, fuel, insurance, etc.
- Reliability—will it break down a lot?
- Longevity—how long will it last?
- Safety to use and repair.
- Availability of parts and servicing.
- Does it do the job that you require of it? How well?

Having decided which tools you really need to buy, follow the guidelines for purchase and maintenance in Chapter 5, 'Gardening and Landscaping Tools', and your equipment should give you good service.

Should you buy, lease or hire?

Often a viable alternative to buying is to lease or hire equipment, either long or short term. These days you can hire most types of garden equipment. You need to have a very clear understanding of what you will be doing in your work and to consider such factors as:

- How often do you use the equipment—why buy when you can hire the equipment on the occasions you need it.
- Up-front capital costs—can you afford to buy the equipment or would it be easier to pay periodical rental or leasing costs?
- Do you have the technical expertise to keep the equipment in good working order—good rental companies keep their equipment well maintained and serviced and will replace equipment that is faulty.
- In many cases the rental hire or lease payments may be tax deductible. Leasing or renting makes it easier to keep up-to-date with new equipment.

DEVELOPING A BUSINESS

No matter what you choose to start with, remember that the modern world is continually changing. Be aware that:

- Whatever business you start today, it is unlikely to be the same in five years time.
- If you want to keep a business viable, you must keep up to date.
- You must know about new technology and new techniques, and adapt whenever it becomes appropriate.

This does *not* mean that you must purchase new equipment every time something better comes onto the market. It does mean that you need to change the way you do things before your competitors get a significant advantage over you. For instance, if everyone else in the lawnmowing business uses modern mowers that mow faster, better, and never break down, while you still use out-of-date equipment, your business will slowly but surely suffer.

Consultation with an accountant who has had a few landscaper clients could be very helpful if you are contemplating starting up a business. Without divulging private details of their clients, an accountant may be able to direct you in how to set up correctly, save money and run more efficiently. While the accountant does not have the actual landscaping knowledge, he or she can offer sound money management expertise.

If you have worked in the industry before as an employee but now wish to expand out on your own, the experience you have gained over the years (contacts, sources, reputation, landscape ability) will be valuable. It is not recommended that you steal clients from your present employer when you move out on your own—this can lead to heated arguments or worse.

Over time, a business may either grow or decline. Very few businesses stay the same size year after year, without change. A business that grows slowly (e.g. 5–20% growth each year) is manageable and likely to be around for a long time.

When a business grows fast (e.g. 200% or more each year) it is much more difficult to manage. The owner can more easily lose control over what is happening and there is a much greater risk of something going wrong.

Chapter 8, 'Managing Finances and Costing' will give you useful insights into the successful running and development of your business.

Manage your growth

If you understand how and where your business has potential to grow, you can then make choices about where you will (and will not) foster growth. Growth can come in any of the following ways:

1. Increasing the quantity of trade

This involves increasing the amount of work, hence the amount of money being turned over each year. Increasing turnover can increase profit, but that is not always the case. For example, a gardening business that has one employee, one car, and one mower might have ample work to keep that person employed full time. If they increase the amount of trade by 10%, they might need to purchase another car, another mower and engage another employee. The extra 10% in earnings probably is not enough to cover the extra equipment costs.

2. Increasing the profitability

By paying closer attention to where you spend money it is often possible to reduce the amount you spend, thus increasing the profit from a business without increasing the amount of annual turnover.

3. Vertical expansion

In the delivery of any service, there is a vertical chain of businesses each contributing to the final service the customer receives. For example, one company builds a machine for earthmoving, a subcontractor buys or hires the machine to do a job, and a landscaper hires the subcontractor to do some earthmoving. If the landscaper expanded vertically, he or she could buy their own machine and eliminate the need to employ the subcontractor.

4. Horizontal expansion

Horizontal expansion may involve expanding the range of services offered, without the vertical expansion outlined above. A landscaper, for example, who had been contracting to construct small gardens only, might start contracting to landscape large gardens as well. This is horizontal expansion.

3
Plant Care

Before going into detail about the various garden services you might consider, let us take a brief overview of plants. You'll be working in their world, and you'll need to understand them in sickness and in health, to anticipate their needs and to know what turns them on and what puts them off. That knowledge is the key to any successful gardening business.

Healthy plants grow stronger, live longer and look better. Everyone wants their plants to be healthy, and with the right plants and the appropriate treatment, there is no reason why all your plants can't look just as good as anything you would buy from a nursery.

When a plant becomes unhealthy, it's usually because the environment is unkind to it. The temperature may be too hot or cold, it might be too wet or dry, it may have too much or too little fertiliser, or perhaps something else is affecting it. Often a sick plant is found to be suffering from attack by a pest or disease problem, but those problems are far more likely to occur with plants that are already suffering because environmental conditions are not suitable.

The first step towards having a good garden is to keep only healthy plants in it. If you are designing a garden for someone, or advising a client on what to plant, consider the following:

- The plants that will prosper are those that are best suited to the particular soil and environment. This might mean some 'terrific' varieties should not be grown, but why grow such plants if they are never going to perform to their peak in that particular environment?
- If the client is determined to grow particular plants that are unsuited to the local environmental conditions, then try to modify those conditions to suit such plants. For example, provide extra shade for shade-loving plants by using shadecloth.
- Be ruthless—get rid of sick plants (or branches) before they become diseased and affect other plants.

Why plants get sick

Plants can get sick just as easily as people. The problems they encounter can include:

Pests. Animals of various sizes and forms (from microscopic worms to dogs, birds, grazing animals, even humans). Insects are just one of many groups of animals that can cause damage to plants, although they are perhaps the most significant group of plant pests.

Diseases. These are problems caused by living organisms other than animals. Fungi, bacteria and virus are the most common.

Environmental disorders. Troubles caused by soils, nutritional problems, poor drainage or bad weather conditions such as frost, wind, cold, heat.

Weeds. Weeds are plants growing where you don't want them. It is the location of a plant that makes it a weed, not the species of the plant. A weed will compete with your desired plants for nutrients, water and space, which can be harmful to your desired plants. They may also act as hosts to pests and diseases that can affect your desired plants.

PREVENTATIVE MEDICINE IN THE GARDEN

The best way to ensure that problems like those outlined above do not occur in gardens you are maintaining is to prevent problems from ever starting. This is best done by following the standard procedures listed below.

1. Consider the site

Does it have any particular problems that should be treated?

- Hard clay soils need to be loosened up by cultivation, or by adding soil conditioners such as lime or gypsum, or by incorporating organic matter such as well-rotted manures and compost.
- Sandy soils can sometimes dry out too easily or be low in nutrients. To overcome these problems add well-rotted manures or compost.
- Wind can make problems. Provide windbreaks, or channel winds with fences or plantings, or provide suitable staking or support until plants are well established.
- Shade caused by large existing trees or buildings calls for special treatment. In such areas select plants that will tolerate or even prefer periods of shade.
- Frost pockets on sloping sites can be removed by planting or fencing in such a way that air movement is allowed to continue unimpeded down the slope.

Other soil problems such as low nutrient levels or diseases may have built up, particularly where the same type of plant has been grown in a particular spot year after year, or the soil may be full of a mat of dead roots. Consider cultivating

The main maintenance tasks for native gardens will involve removal of fallen limbs, clearing paths, collecting fallen leaves and the occasional plant trimming.

and building up the soil, and replanting with different types of plants that are not susceptible to any of the diseases that may be present.

2. Build up the soil

Before you even start a new garden, make sure the soil is in top condition. Ensure that drainage, nutrition and the structure of the soil is suitable for the plants you wish to grow (it should be crumbly and easily worked). This may involve laying drainage pipes, applying fertilisers, gypsum (to help improve structure in heavy soils) or lime, or digging in manure and compost (to improve structure and nutrients). Kill existing soil pests or weeds first if you have any particularly serious problems.

3. Use healthy plants/seeds

Healthy plants are more likely to resist damage from pests and diseases, and have a better chance of surviving if they are attacked. When choosing plants, make sure that the roots and top growth are well developed. There should be no

Formal gardens with shaped plants will need regular clipping.

deformed growths (e.g. twisted, distorted leaves, swellings on roots). Avoid plants with badly marked leaves. Don't use plants contaminated with insects. Seeds and bulbs should be fresh and free of abnormal markings or any rots.

Don't compromise on quality. Trying to save a little money by buying plants that are not in top condition will cost you a lot more in the long term through plant losses and higher maintenance requirements, not to mention the damage to your reputation.

Prefer varieties that are resistant to diseases/pests and are known to be successful in the locality of your client's property. Look around local gardens and see what grows best.

4. *Maintain cleanliness*
- Remove any diseased fruit, flowers, leaves or other plant parts, and burn them. Do not compost them or let them lie on the ground!
- Wash soil off paths and concrete areas. Soil tracked from one area to another may spread diseases.

- Sit potted plants on stones or paving, or on top of a couple of bricks (not directly on top of soil). This minimises movement of disease from the soil up into the pot.
- Be careful not to wear dirty boots into a propagation area—they can carry diseases from the general garden into the propagation area.
- Hoses and their fittings should be neatly stored so that they are not in contact with the ground, otherwise they can pick up diseases easily and spread them rapidly when used.
- All tools should be regularly cleaned of soil and other debris. Tools used for cutting plant tissue should be regularly disinfected (e.g. dipped in 'metho' or a disinfectant such as Dettol).

5. Maintain plant nutrition and water
Do not overwater or underwater—each is as bad as the other!

Overwatering(waterlogging) is indicated by yellowing of the lower leaves, sometimes wilting and eventually dropping of the lower leaves.

Underwatering is indicated by browning of the tips and foliage generally, and at times by severe wilting and leaf drop.

Lack of nutrients is indicated by a slow rate of growth and, in severe cases, by discolouration patterns on leaves.

Troubleshoot quickly
Inspect plants regularly, looking at the tips first. The young growth will indicate general vigour (or lack of it). Look for dieback, discolouration of leaves or wood, distortion of growth, rots, eaten or broken tissue.

Planting

A plant that is planted well will become established quicker and be more likely to thrive in the long term. Before planting be sure that the site selected for the plants is well prepared—it should have suitable drainage, be well cultivated and, ideally, have plenty of well-rotted organic matter and perhaps some fertiliser added.

Basic planting procedure
Plant most containerised plants as follows:
1. Thoroughly soak the plant in the pot, so that the plant will come out of the pot easily, and allow it to drain.
2. Dig a hole at least one-and-a-half times the depth of the pot.
3. Place a little fertiliser in the hole.
4. Backfill one third of the hole and mix the fertiliser with the backfilled soil.
5. Carefully take the plant out of the pot.
6. Loosen any exposed roots. If most of the roots are inside the soil ball, you

might not need to do much; if there is a tight mass of roots on the outside of the soil ball you may need to break a centimetre or so into the ball all over. Free any roots circling the bottom.

7. Place the plant in the hole and cover with soil. The top of the original soil from the container should be level with the surrounding ground level, or only lightly covered. Firm the soil down around the plant, but don't pack it down.
8. Make a small lip of soil around the base of the plant to hold water.
9. Soak thoroughly with water.

Fertiliser

You can get concentrated, fast-acting fertilisers that will feed more nutrients to the plant, very quickly, or slower acting, long-term fertilisers ... and there are many possibilities in between these two extremes. Avoid direct contact between the roots of a young plant and the stronger fertilisers. Usually a slower acting fertiliser is more appropriate with planting, particularly in sandy soils. Blood and bone, Osmocote, or something similar is ideal for planting most plants.

Staking

Staking is not always necessary; in fact, it can in some cases do more harm than good. Plants should be staked if they are likely to fall over (perhaps because they are exposed to severe winds, perhaps because they are loose in the soil). Plants might be staked to protect them from vandalism or unintentional damage, although you may need to consider whether stakes will draw attention to a plant, perhaps attracting vandals.

When you do tie a plant to a stake the tie should be loose, allowing the plant to move about in the wind. If movement is restricted, the tree may never develop proper strength in its trunk or in the join between the roots and trunk. Tying materials should be soft so that they do not damage the trunk of the plant (materials such as hessian strips or old pantyhose are effective).

Bare-rooted plants

These include such things as deciduous trees and roses and, occasionally, perennials and herbs. When handling a bare-rooted plant it is essential to keep the roots protected from drying out. Store plants in a container filled with moist wood shavings. Before you plant, examine the roots carefully. Any swellings are best cut off (these may be due to disease). If you cut the roots back for this or any other reason, cut the top back proportionally. It is good practice to dust with benlate or some other fungicide.

When planting bare-rooted plants dig a hole large enough to allow you to make a slight mound in the centre. The plant is then placed centrally over the mound and its roots positioned as evenly as possible around the plant and directed over and down the slope of the mound. This encourages the roots to go downwards a little rather than directly outwards, making the plant more stable, and the roots less likely to dry out in hard conditions. Staking may also be necessary to provide initial support. The stake should be placed in position prior to the plant being placed in the hole to ensure that roots aren't damaged, as might occur if the stake were driven in after the plant was in position.

Time of planting

Avoid planting on hot or windy days. Plants are more likely to dry out in these conditions. Deciduous trees are usually planted in winter (as are all bare-rooted plants), because it is at this time of the year that these trees are released to the nurseries for sale. This is because these plants are generally dormant at this stage, and transplant shock will usually be only minimal. They are also easier to transport and handle without their leaves.

If plants are likely to get a lot of attention, they can be planted successfully at almost any time of year; however, if they are likely to be neglected they are best planted prior to the cooler months or wetter time of the year, allowing them to become established before the harsher months. If planting in warm areas where the wetter months are over summer, such as the northern parts of Australia, you can plant almost any time of the year as long as you provide sufficient moisture during dry times and good drainage during wet periods.

Moving established plants

Moving established plants may become necessary when redesigning an existing garden, where plants are in inappropriate positions, or perhaps if house extensions are being built. Many plants can be readily transplanted, particularly when they are small. For best results the following factors should be considered.

- A plant is more likely to survive transplanting if it is in good condition. Simply maintaining good plant health through watering, feeding, pruning, etc. will give a plant a much greater chance of survival. This applies both before and after transplanting.
- Plants can be prepared several months in advance if you know that they will need shifting. Using a sharp-bladed spade, simply push it into the ground about the spade head deep, in a circle around the plant to be shifted. The distance from the trunk of the plant that you make this circle will depend on how big a rootball you intend to take—the bigger the rootball the better, but for larger plants it becomes impracticable to take too big a rootball, as it would become too difficult to lift out and transport. Slicing the outer, near-surface roots in this manner encourages a mass of fibrous roots to develop before transplanting actually takes place. This reduces the likelihood of transplant shock and allows the plant to re-establish more quickly in its new position.
- Take as much of the rootball as possible when transplanting. The less you disturb the roots the better.

- Trim any exposed, jaggedly cut roots with a sharp, clean pair of secateurs. Top growth of the plant may need to be trimmed back to minimise water loss and reduce the likelihood of the plant blowing over, particularly if the root ball has been heavily reduced.
- Timing is important. Deciduous plants are usually best transplanted in winter when they are dormant. Evergreens are usually best planted when growing conditions are best (e.g. spring and autumn). Avoid hot and windy days when transplanting, to minimise stress on the plant.
- Carefully prepare the area where the plant is to be re-established by cultivating and fertilising well, adding well-rotted organic matter and providing good drainage where appropriate.
- Be sure the plant won't fall or blow over once it has been replanted. Usually some form of staking is required until the plant has re-established.
- Make sure you continue to maintain the plant once it has been replanted, at least until you are sure it has become established in its new position.

Tree guards

These are sometimes used to protect plants from foraging rabbits, kangaroos, or farm animals by providing a physical barrier between the plant and the animal. Tree guards are also good in deterring vandalism of treasured plants. Some guards offer complete protection from wind and sun, while others allow air and filtered sunlight to reach the plant. The choice of the tree guard will depend upon the plant, the growth rate, the pest to be deterred, and the cost and durability.

Feeding plants

If inadequate nutrients are present in the soil, plant growth is stunted. This effect is subtle and not usually noticed until it becomes severe. Plant nutrient use can drop to as low as 30% of optimum levels before deficiency symptoms, such as discolouration, appear in the leaves. By this time, the overall growth rate and general health of the plant has been affected significantly. Every plant variety has its own unique set of nutrient requirements: some plants need more iron and less phosphorus than others, some need more phosphorus and less potassium. There are tens of thousands of different 'ideal' nutrient conditions—one for each different plant!

Too much fertiliser can do more harm than good. It may even burn a plant. To avoid this, never allow fertiliser (even dust) to get onto the leaves and always carefully follow the instructions on a fertiliser packet. Table 3.1 will be a reliable guide to fertiliser use.

TABLE 3.1. WHAT FERTILISER TO USE WHERE

FERTILISER TYPE	HOW IT WORKS	WHERE TO USE IT
Slow release granules (e.g. Nutricote, Osmocote)	Nutrients are released slowly through a surface coating over a long period	Planting new trees/ shrubs. In a potting mix. Existing lawns & gardens. Hanging baskets.
Pelleted fertiliser (e.g. Dynamic Lifter)	Nutrients release more slowly from a solid lump than from a powder	Planting new trees/ shrubs. Existing lawns & gardens. Fruit trees and vegetables.
Organic liquid food (e.g. Maxicrop, Nitrosol)	Its organic nature slows nutrient release, but its solubility allows faster release than solid organic fertilisers	Regular feeding of pot plants. Annuals, vegetables, herbs in established beds
Powdered organic food (e.g. blood & bone, hoof & horn)	Gradual break-down, releasing nutrients over several months	Preparing a vegetable or flower garden or garden bed. Around plants mulched with organic material to compensate for nitrogen loss
General powder-like inorganic fertilisers (e.g. sulphate of ammonia, potash)	Generally dissolve in water and are either used fast or are leached through the soil and lost	Giving a boost to feeding during rapid growth. Quickly correcting a detected nutrient deficiency.

In general, many gardeners over-fertilise, particularly if they fertilise once or twice a year with large amounts of fertiliser. Fast-acting fertilisers (e.g. sulphate of ammonia), which can be easily leached from the soil, are best used more regularly and in lighter doses. This will allow plants to utilise as much of the fertiliser as possible before it is leached away.

Timing is also important. It is not much use using fertilisers during periods when plants are not actively growing. For example, fertilising many plants in winter in Southern Australia is usually a total waste. For slower release fertilisers, less frequent applications can be made, as the nutrients are slowly released over a longer period of time. Be careful, however, not to oversupply such fertilisers.

Watering

Water is essential for good plant growth. All plants need water to grow and to survive but the amount of water needed will vary from plant to plant.
The two main factors affecting how much water a plant needs are:

1. The variety of the plant. Some types of plants have the ability to retain water within their tissues for later use; others are unable to do this.

2. The environment in which the plant is growing. If there is plenty of water available around the plant, then it is unlikely to suffer from a lack of water. Shaded, cool situations tend to remain moister than exposed, windy, sunny situations. A plant can suffer from a lack of water; it can also suffer from an excessive amount of water. When you water a plant it is important to strike that delicate balance between too little and too much. Overwatering can be just as bad as underwatering, resulting in poor growth and/or encouraging the spread of pests and diseases, particularly root rots.

Formal gardens such as this require high maintenance.

Too little water
- The first symptom is usually that the rate of growth slows. This is usually a mild case, only a slight deficiency.
- Stems become slender, leaves become smaller, flowers and fruit become smaller.
- If a plant that has a watery type of fruit (such as a tomato) is under-watered, it can begin to take moisture out of the fruit, i.e. the tomatoes begin to shrivel.
- Wilting.
- In extreme water deficiency, the tips of the plant can die back and perhaps the whole plant might die.

Too much water
- Seedlings can become leggy if they are planted close together in a nursery, and if there is too much moisture about.
- Plant tissue cells can become enlarged and in extreme cases they might burst.
- Internodes become elongated, ie: the spaces between two leaves on a stem become greater than normal.
- In some situations yellowing of foliage may occur because plants are unable to obtain as much nitrogen in waterlogged conditions. This commonly occurs in poorly drained lawns.
- In extreme situations leaves can blacken and the plant can die back or die off completely.

Sufficient water
Consider the soil where a plant is growing. If a plant is getting too wet, perhaps the soil should be better drained; if it is getting too dry, perhaps the soil should have a better capacity to retain moisture. Other things to consider are:

- *Frequency of watering:* Maybe you need to water more often, or less.
- *Water penetration:* Does the water you apply infiltrate the soil or does it run off and get lost? Does it land on the leaves of plants, thus being deflected away from the soil? Does the sun or wind remove it before the plant can use it?
- *The plant's position:* Is the plant in a shaded situation? Is it in a very hot situation? How much natural rainfall has it been getting?

These problems can all be rectified. You just need to know that there is a problem in the first place.

Watering equipment
There is a wide range of watering equipment for the garden, from watering cans, hoses and moveable sprinklers to all types of fixed irrigation systems.

If your client lives in a flat or unit, a watering can may very well be all you need for a few indoor plants or tub plants on a verandah. For larger gardens, however, some sort of permanent irrigation system is ideal.

Hoses come in all types and sizes. Less expensive hoses will often start to crack and develop leaks after a year or so, particularly if left outside in direct sunlight. Generally, more expensive reinforced hoses are a better product and will last much longer.

Clip-on hose fittings are today available in a variety of sizes, allowing you to easily attach or detach different connections.

Irrigation systems generally come in one of four types:

• **Drip irrigation** provides a very slow trickle or drip of water, and because they water slower they tend to water deeper. Watering does not need to be done so often, and water is not wasted so much through excess run off or by watering unnecessary places. Diseases of the foliage are generally less likely to occur, as the foliage remains drier.

• **Micro-spray irrigation**. These are small, inexpensive plastic moulded spray heads, which can be purchased individually or in kit form, and easily attached to risers from 'poly ' pipe (usually 13 or 19 mm diameter). Most gardeners can install this type of system with little effort.

• **Fixed above-ground sprinklers.** This involves very solid (usually metal) sprinkler heads set in a fixed position above ground. Suited to garden beds, or along the edge of a path or wall, or in fruit and vegetable growing areas. This type of system is much more expensive, can look unsightly in some situations, and requires a much higher level of expertise to install.

• **Pop-up sprinklers** are well suited to lawns, where they can sink below the surface, out of sight, when not in operation. Some cheaper pop-ups can occasionally remain stuck up out of the ground and get in the way of lawn mowers. Be aware of this when mowing. They can be readily installed, even in existing lawns, and are relatively inexpensive.

How to manually handle objects in the garden

Some simple techniques can prevent a lot of the injuries that are common as a result of manual handling of objects. This applies to many gardening tools that are commonly used.

• Always bend your knees and keep your back straight when reaching down to pick up something.
• Don't attempt to lift anything that may be to heavy for you. Try rocking the object first to get an indication of its weight. Get help if there is any doubt about whether you can easily lift the object.
• Use work gloves and safety boots, particularly if the object could have sharp or rough-surfaced parts, where insects or spiders may be present, and just in case you drop the darned thing.

- Don't over-exert yourself or put yourself in a position where you can overbalance. This applies particularly when straining to use such tools as rakes, shovels, crowbars and heavy mechanical equipment.

4
Garden Maintenance Services

A garden maintenance business provides services that help to maintain the general health or condition and the presentation of a garden. These services might include such things as lawnmowing, lawn repair and renovation, pruning, spraying pesticides, fertilising or soil care, replacing old or sick plants, maintaining indoor plants, tree lopping or tree surgery.

There was a time when anyone could start this type of business and as long as they were prepared to do physical work, and sweat a little, they would have a reasonable chance of success. Garden maintenance today is, however, becoming more sophisticated and increasingly mechanised. If you are to do jobs as well as your competition, you must have some basic knowledge, but very often you also need the right machinery or you will simply take longer to do a job, and sooner or later the clients will discover that they can get more for their money by employing a better equipped gardener.

Many home and business owners will contact their local nursery to obtain gardening services, or pay extra to have plants installed rather than digging and planting themselves. Contracting your services through a nursery is a good starting point for a new garden maintenance business, or it can be an opportunity for an existing business.

PROVIDING A SPRAYING SERVICE

A chemical and pesticide spraying service can be a very viable business venture. Many home owners choose to employ people to spray pests in their garden when problems become extreme, if they don't want to handle and store chemicals themselves. Others elect to adopt chemical control as part of their regular garden maintenance. There are also lots of possibilities providing spraying services for farmers, as well as government and commercial properties, where there is often the need to employ people to spray for weeds and other problems on a routine basis. New building construction sites, sports fields and many other areas requiring immediate weed and/or pest treatment would also be potential customers for a spraying service.

While the possibilities for this type of business are very lucrative, you need to be continually aware of what is occurring in the industry and of the need to exercise the utmost care at all times. Many toxic chemicals are banned outright, or are only allowed for use in specific areas. There are also often strict regulations/laws in regard to what areas can be sprayed (e.g. spraying may not be allowed within a set distance from schools and children's play areas) and in regard to legal liability, such as with spray drifting. There is also a trend toward the use of natural means of pest and weed control, and a policy of zero runoff from all properties is to be in place by the year 2000.

The start-up costs for a spraying service would include: public liability insurance, high quality equipment, licences for application and handling of a range of chemicals, protective gear for operators, etc. as well as the usual business start-up costs. (See Chapter 5, Table 5.1, for a comparison of spraying equipment). While this makes the cost of entry into this sector very high, it also makes it less competitive than many other landscape and gardening businesses.

Using chemicals

Let us look at the various methods of applying chemicals:

Spraying

The chemical is mixed into a solution and sprayed onto the plant or soil. This is relatively easy to do with the right equipment and spreads the chemical evenly, which is important if it is to do the job. However, it can have a few problems:

- On a wet day, the rain dilutes the chemical and that may affect the result. So don't spray on wet days!
- On a hot day, moisture can evaporate quickly, making the spray more concentrated, which can affect the job and maybe even burn the plant. So don't spray on a hot day!
- On a windy day spray mist can drift. It can blow on you or other people, causing poisoning. It can blow into neighbouring properties, affecting plants, animals or even insects that you don't want to harm. So don't spray on winday days, either!
- In liquid form, chemicals are more readily absorbed into your skin, particularly if you are sweating. Be careful!

Dusting

This involves blowing or shaking a fine powder over plants. The major problem is in windy weather, when more of the chemical can end up off the plants than on them.

Granules

There are chemicals that are sprinkled on the soil and gradually break down with

Spraying for pests, disease and weeds will require the right spray equipment, such as knapsacks.

rain or watering to move into the plant's roots. Only certain types of chemicals work this way:

- Solid fertilisers.
- Granular insecticides and fungicides that are absorbed into the roots of a plant and moved through the plant's sap system (e.g. Disyston).
- Granular chemicals which kill disease spores, insects or weed seeds that are in the soil and may at a later stage affect the plant.

With irrigation (through a sprinkler system)

Some chemicals can be added to the irrigation system and sprayed onto plants through sprinklers or dripped onto the roots through drippers. Only certain types of chemicals are suited to this method of application. Such chemicals need to act quickly, because the irrigation which applies them will also wash them away from the plant.

Injection

This involves directly pouring or injecting a chemical into the sap system of a plant. It is by far the safest method of applying chemicals because it cannot drift or spread to places away from the plant. Unfortunately, this method only works with chemicals that have the ability to move through the sap system of the plant. Its main use is for treating large trees.

Warning. Trees subject to browsing by animals or stock should not be treated. Children should not be allowed to come in contact with the chemical. Fruit trees should not be treated.

Golden rules for using chemicals

1. Only use chemicals when actually needed!
2. Use the correct chemical for the job at hand; if unsure; seek advice.
3. *Always* read the label *and* the product information sheets (if available).
4. Use protective clothing at *all* times. For some chemicals this may involve rubber gloves. For many chemicals, however, face masks and spray suits may be required.
5. Use the correct pesticide application equipment, and be sure the equipment is properly cleaned and maintained.
6. Don't spray on windy or very hot days, or when rainfall is imminent.
7. Warn other people in the area that you are going to spray (and have sprayed).
8. Wash out all spray equipment thoroughly when finished, being sure to dispose of the wash water in a recommended manner.
9. Do not eat or smoke while spraying.
10. Wash all protective clothing thoroughly after spraying.
11. Wash yourself thoroughly after spraying, especially the hands.
12. Store spray equipment and chemicals in a safe, locked place. Be sure to store chemicals in their original containers.
13. Dispose of empty pesticide containers according to the label instructions.
14. Record all details of your spraying.

STARTING A PRUNING SERVICE

One thing is a certain in any garden: plants will grow too big and people will want them pruned. Pruning does require skill, though. Not all plants are pruned the same way, or with the same equipment. Small to medium pruning jobs can be done with little investment in equipment.

The pruning work we are discussing here does not include those jobs normally done by a skilled arborculturist, including tree felling, large branch removal and tree cabling. These jobs need special expertise and to attempt these large jobs without proper training and equipment can cause damage to the tree, to buildings and to yourself.

Pruning can also be very seasonal work, particularly in cooler temperate regions, such as the southern states of Australia. Consider combining such a service with another seasonal work area, such as lawnmowing, which will keep you busy when there's not much pruning work around.

If you intend to provide a pruning service, make sure you are always very clear and specific about what will be provided with the service. Many clients will expect that cartage and disposal of the pruned plants will be included in the price. Many councils now charge for tip disposal, burning off can be strictly limited, and some wood simply doesn't burn well. Chipping and using the wood for mulching is an alternative way to dispose of the materials.

How to prune

Plants are pruned for all sorts of reasons, and the way to prune a plant depends upon what you want from the plant and where you are. Roses, for instance, need to be pruned very hard in colder climates to achieve the best flowering, but similar treatment in the sub-tropics can result in a very poor crop of flowers.

Gardeners are less definite today about the best method to prune a rose, shrub or fruit tree than they were twenty years ago. In the past, many plants were pruned in the traditional shape of an inverted cone (particularly roses and fruit trees). Experiments have show that other shapes can be just as productive and as visually effective as this traditional shape.

With better watering, fertilising and weed control, plants are able to carry a lot more flowers and fruit than they could a few decades ago. Consequently, the detailed heavy pruning of the past is not always practised nowadays.

In the home garden, pruning is mainly done to shape the plant so that it fits into the general function and design of the overall garden.

Pruning preparation

Prior to pruning, look closely at the plant or tree and try to understand how it grows. What parts of the tree produce flowers and fruit, what shape do you want to achieve, and do you want large flowers or fruit?

Deciduous trees and garden plants are usually pruned in winter as the plants are bare of leaves and at that time it is easier to see what you are cutting.

Note the size of the buds. Larger, plump buds are flower/fruit buds. Narrower buds are vegetative (i.e. they produce only leaves or green shoots). The number of flower buds will give an indication of the amount of fruit the tree is likely to bear. (Note: On some types of trees, one bud can produce several fruit; on others one bud produces only one fruit). You will notice that fruit buds are borne on particular parts of a tree; for instance, peaches bear fruit on one-year-old laterals whereas apples bear fruit on the tips of one-year-old laterals and also in small clusters of compact growths called 'spur systems'.

The basis of your pruning should be to cut in a way that will encourage the development of the type of growth which will produce flowers, fruit and/or shape for future years, but at the same time leave enough buds to allow a reasonable crop (in the case of fruit or flowers) for the coming season.

Pruning considerations

- The vigour of the plant or shoot depends on the direction of growth and the amount of leaf surface (among other things).
- The more a shoot approaches the vertical position, the stronger its growth will be.
- The top or terminal bud of a shoot generally has the greatest amount of growth. The growth potential of the buds will gradually decrease as you come closer to the base of a shoot.
- The greater the leaf (vegetative) growth, the lighter the crop, resulting in larger but poorer quality flowers or fruit.
- The fewer the buds on a shoot, the stronger will be the growth made by each individual shoot arising from these buds.
- All flowers and fruit should be removed from young fruit plants for the first few years after planting, to allow the leaf and stem growth to better develop.

Pruning technique

Start by cutting out the dead wood and crossing limbs, then identify the bud that you wish to remain on the plant that is pointing in the direction in which you want growth to go. You will need to remove the excess plant material above that bud.

Generally, an angled cut is made above the bud so that the high part of the cut is above the bud and the low part of the cut is on the other side of the stem. It is important not to cut too close to the bud otherwise it may die. If you cut too far away from the bud, the stem may suffer from die-back and make the stem disease prone and can lead to death of that stem. If the cut is of a large branch, consider using a wound dressing to seal the cut.

Cutting large branches

When large branches are to be pruned (referred to as tree surgery), the first objective is to remove most of the branch's weight. You can then make a clean final cut without the risk of the weight causing a tear.

Firstly, cut on the underside of the branch about 50 cm away from the intended final prune. Make this first cut upwards into the limb for about a quarter its width. The second cut is made a little further away from the final cut, about 70cm along the limb. The final cut is made downwards all the way through, or until the branch falls off. The purpose of the first undercut is to prevent bark ripping off the trunk. Now you should be left with a branch about 70 cm long, which is easier to work with.

The final prune of a limb should be at the point where the limb naturally forms a swollen area at its junction with the trunk. This may be cut in any direction, but always try to prevent bark ripping. Seal with a wound dressing.

It is wise wherever possible to use prunings in your client's garden. The best way is to compost the prunings. First, however, these will need to be shredded into smaller pieces to aid the decomposition process. Many companies now make shredders and clippers within a reasonable price range for everyone. Large branches may possibly be used for landscaping as fences, retaining walls or garden furniture.

TABLE 4.1. HOW TO PRUNE SOME POPULAR PLANTS

PLANT	SEASON	TECHNIQUE
Abelia	Winter	Remove some older branches each year near ground for rejuvenation
Azalea	Spring/Summer	After flowering, for shape
Bougainvillea	Summer	After flowers, to control shape and size
Bulbs	Varies	Remove foliage after it dies down
Callistemon	Summer	Remove spent flowers after flowering to improve next season's growth
Deciduous fruit trees (apple, pear, peach, apricot, etc.)	Summer	Prune to control excessive growth and limbs that may damage fruit.
	Winter	Prune to thin out existing fruit buds and stimulate new growth that will carry fruit next year
Grevilleas	Varies	Tip prune after flowering to encourage a flush of new growth that will carry next crop of flowers
Lemon	Autumn	Prune for shape and to remove limbs that may damage fruit or are dead or diseased
Perennials (aster, chrysanthemum, many rock plants)	Autumn	Remove old top growth prior to dormant period
	Winter	Hard prune to vase shape in cold areas; medium prune in warmer areas
Roses	Throughout year	Tip prune after flowering to maintain shape.

Pruning equipment

Secateurs

Secateurs are an essential tool for any gardener. There are two main types:
'Parrot' type—two curved cutting blades which cut with a scissor action;
'Anvil' type—one cutting blade, one soft metal anvil. The cut is made by the sharp blade coming down on top of the flat anvil.

Keep secateurs well maintained, cleaned and oiled. Never cut too large a stem, or twist the tool when trying to cut a thick stem. Most brands supply individuals blades for replacements.

Long-arm pruners and shears

These are used to prune plant material that is out of the reach of secateurs.
Long-arm pruners consist of a swivelling blade that cuts onto an anvil. Quality of cut is not as good as secateurs but the advantage lies in strength and reach.
Shears are similar in design to secateurs but they have longer handles which provide greater leverage and strength.

Saws

Saws are used to cut larger branch material that cannot be cut by secateurs or pruners. Care must be taken when using saws and other pruning tools, as injury can occur with improper use. Saws can have either of two blade designs:
Cross-cut saws are normally used for tree work, being designed to cut across the grain.
Ripper saws are designed to cut with or down the grain.

Roses are generally pruned this severely in winter in temperate climates, but less severely in warm climates.

There are six types of saws:

1. Hand saw—frequently used for tree work and the home garden.
2. Tubular frame saw—used for cutting up fallen prunings. Limited use for prune cutting trees due to its rough cut.
3. Pruning saw—designed for use in narrow angles and small gaps between branches. May be either single- or double-edged. A double-edged saw has course double teeth on one side for large branches and soft wood when a wide cut is needed, and fine peg teeth on the other side.
4. Grecian pruning saw—cuts on drawing stroke, i.e. as the operator draws the tool towards himself. Because it has a very good grip and pointed blade it is useful for the gardener and landscaper.
5. Long-arm saw—cuts on drawing stroke. Similar in design to Grecian saw except that it has a longer handle for reaching awkward areas.
6. One-man and two-man cross-cut saws—these saws are designed for falling large trees and cutting timbers. They have generally been superseded by chainsaws.

Shredders, mulchers and chippers

These machines convert garden prunings into mulch and compost material. For the serious gardener and environmentally aware home owner, this is almost as important as the mower. In fact you can sometimes use the mower to shred up small pruning materials. For large twigs or for large quantities, a shredder is essential. Each piece of equipment on the market has its advantages, so it is

Prunings can be chipped—this reduces refuse from the garden and produces mulch at the same time.

best to contact your local suppliers for further information.

As with many other tools and machines, you get what you pay for. Small 1–2 horsepower machines are valuable but do not handle thick branches and are very slow to get through the work for a medium to large garden. Such machines can be purchased for a few hundred dollars, but what you save on the purchase price you may lose on the extra time you spend getting through the mulching. For disposing of the prunings from the average to large home garden a 4–8 horsepower machine is what is really needed, but that will cost anything from $1 000 to $4 000.

STARTING A LAWN CARE BUSINESS

Lawn care and grass cutting services are very popular small businesses. Almost everyone knows how to safely and efficiently use a lawn mower, either through having a 'mowing route' as a youngster or through care of their own lawn. The start-up costs are quite low, as only a mower, trailer, fuel and car or truck are necessary to get started.

As with all other gardening services, you need to be careful to specify what services are included for the cost quoted. For instance, you may quote to mow a lawn, intending to provide trimming around trees once a month, while the home owner may expect that service weekly. A lawnmowing service does not have to include garden maintenance, and any such additional services should be specified in your original agreement.

In the southern states, where lawnmowing is a seasonal need, a lawn care service might be a great combination with a cool season service, such as pruning.

Cutting grass

A lawn mower is usually the first piece of garden machinery a person buys. There are many different types of grass cutting machines, man powered or machine powered; some you ride on and others you walk behind.

The cheapest mowers available are push-type cylinder mowers, and for a small lawn they can give an excellent cut if you don't mind exercising a bit of muscle occasionally. Electric mowers are cheaper than petrol mowers, but they can be dangerous if you run over the power lead, and repairs are not usually so straightforward if you develop problems with the engine. Two-stroke petrol mowers are generally cheaper than four-stroke mowers.

Not all mowers will do the same job, so it is important that you purchase the right one for your situation When buying a mower consider the size of the land, the slope and undulations of the terrain, quality of the land (stones, clayey), quality of cut, whether mowing will need to be carried out while wet, etc.

Cutting action

Mowers cut grass in one of four different ways:

1. *Scissor cut*. Cuts by the action of two blades moving across each other like a pair of scissors. It is sometimes used by councils for slashing very long grass, but rarely used in the home garden.
2. *Rotary cut*. Cuts with a sharpened blade rotating horizontally and hitting the grass at a 90° angle. This can damage grass, isn't as good on quality lawns, and doesn't cut well in the wet.
3. *Cylinder-mounted blades*. Cuts by a rotating cylinder containing blades which hit the grass on a 45° angle. This provides a much better quality cut, doesn't tear the grass and will cut better when the grass is wet.
4. *Gangs*. Several mowers (usually rotary or cylinder) mounted side by side to give a wider cut.

Power source

The power source is worth noting, as it can indicate the amount of human energy needed to operate the mower. Mowers can be powered by:

- Man power (push type)
- Electricity
- 2-stroke motor
- 4-stroke motor
- Power Take Off (PTO) from a tractor or similar machine. An advantage of the PTO is that it can power other things also (e.g. rotary hoe).

Grass collection

Grass can be either left to lie on the ground or picked up after cutting. The advantages of collecting lawn clippings are:

- Grass is not walked inside the house.
- Clippings do not blow about and make a mess.
- Clippings can be taken away and composted.

It is important to note that the removal process actually takes nutrients from the turf. These need to be replaced periodically with extra feeding or topdressing.

The advantage in leaving clippings on the lawn is that they will compost back into the soil, which benefits very poor soils that are sandy or heavy clay and low in organic content.

Unfortunately if clippings are always left, an oversupply of 'thatch' may occur which can lead to the deterioration and possible death of the lawn.

Width and speed of cut

This determines how much ground can be covered, an important factor if you have large areas of grass. For ride-on mowers which have a wider cutting area and are fast you will then need to consider turning circle and manoeuvrability around trees, posts etc. If the ground is uneven, a wide cutting mower's blades may shave the grass, resulting in an unsightly lawn. For gang or wide cutting mowers a series of 'floating' cylinders are better than one wide slasher.

Mower safety rules

- Don't start up or run a mower in a confined space (e.g. a closed shed) as the exhaust gases produced are poisonous.
- Make sure there are guards on blades to stop material being thrown up and to stop body parts being caught in blades.
- Wear protective clothing and goggles while mowing.
- Do not lift or work on the undercarriage unless the mower is turned off, and preferably with the ignition system disconnected.
- Don't allow inexperienced children (or teenagers) to operate power mowers unsupervised.
- Always be sure the lawn is clear of sticks, stones, toys or any other loose material before mowing.
- Store mower fuel in a cool place, away from any flames such as a gas heater or hot water cylinder. Keep in a container specially designed for mower fuel, and always label the container. Plastic containers are *not* suitable.
- Never smoke when near a mower.

Lawn clippings if left too long in one place can start to decompose and damage the turf it is sitting on. Clippings should be removed promptly.

How to mow—the rules

1. Never mow wet grass with a rotary mower.
2. Avoid mowing wet grass with a cylinder mower.
3. When the grass is long cut it higher. You might cut it a second time (lower) a few days later.
4. Cut twice weekly when grass is growing fast.
5. Cut every 2–3 weeks if grass is growing slowly.
6. Cut grass up to 4 cm tall when not growing fast (e.g. under drought conditions or in cool weather).
7. Never cut grass shorter than 1 cm high (if you want it to remain healthy).
8. Clean sticks, stones or other rubbish off the lawn before mowing.
9. Mow backwards and forwards across the lawn in parallel lines and at right angles to the lines you followed on your previous cut.
10. Avoid mowing on days of extreme heat or cold (this can scorch the cut tips of grass).

Mowers

Cylinder mowers

These are the top quality machines and are generally more expensive than rotary mowers. They are generally designed to cut short to give a very smooth surface, so blades can be damaged on poor (stony or rough) ground. The main parts are:

- Front roller—can be raised or lowered to adjust cutting height.
- Rear rollers—propel the mower.
- Cutting cylinder—cutting blades on cylinder move against the bottom blade to give the cut. Cylinder is driven by a chain, or gears taken off the motor.
- Bottom blade.

Ride-on mowers

There are many different types of ride-on mowers on the market, some of which are notorious for breaking down. Generally you get what you pay for—the cheaper machines may not last a lot of years. You are strongly advised to shop around and talk to people who have used ride-ons before. Talk to several different mower repair shops. You might also get some useful advice from your local parks department.

Ride-ons are not very manoeuvrable in tight corners (e.g. around trees) and can cause compaction on heavy, wet soils. You will almost certainly need a hand mower or brushcutter to cut inaccessible places. The ride-ons, however, are fast and will save a great deal of time and effort on larger properties.

Deciding what you need

Most small to average domestic gardens would use a mower with a cutting width of 30–35 cm. Large properties may require a much larger mower.

TABLE 4.2. MOWER CUTTING WIDTHS

Area you can mow in 1 hour	Cutting width required
800 square metres	30 centimetres
1600 square metres	40 centimetres
2400 square metres	60 centimetres

- Cylinder mowers are safer to use than rotary or hover mowers.
- Two- or four-stroke motor mowers are safer to use than electric mowers.
- Rotary mowers cut overgrown grass better than cylinder or hover types. If you are mowing irregularly, a rotary motor mower is probably best.
- Front-mounted catchers are the most efficient for catching lawn clippings.
- Self-propelled or hover mowers require less physical effort to move over the lawn.
- The more complex the machine, the more that can go wrong with it. Self-propelled, ride-on and four-stroke cylinder mowers are susceptible to a greater range of problems than a basic two-stroke rotary.

Scalping is caused by mowing at too low a height setting.

Mower maintenance

Four-stroke cylinder mowers
- The distance between the cylinder and the bottom blade is critical. If it is correct, it will cut a piece of paper cleanly.
- The bottom blade must be parallel with the cylinder, or excess wear will occur.
- Keep grass and any other rubbish away from engine cooling fins or other engine parts. Clean the mower down after use.
- Leave the petrol tap turned off when the mower is not in use; if left on, it can sometimes make starting more difficult later on.
- Remove and clean the air filter regularly.
- Check the oil every time you mow.
- Change the oil after every 50 hours of use.
- Clean and reset spark plug every 200 hours of use.
- Check drive mechanism regularly, i.e. tension on belt, clutch operation, etc.
- Lubricate moving parts, particularly the cylinder and roller bearings.

Two-stroke rotary mowers
- Check that blades are not damaged or loose. Replace when worn.
- Remove blades and sharpen to increase their life, but don't overheat blades on the grindstone.
- Keep grass and rubbish away from vents, cooling fins or other engine parts.
- Petrol tap is best left off.
- Keep air filter clean.
- Oil is mixed into petrol, so it is not necessary to check oil.
- Clean spark plugs often—once a month is ideal.

Electric motor mowers
- Check power cord and plug, replace damaged cables.
- Check blades, make sure they are in good condition.
- Keep the mower clean, top and bottom. Make sure all wet grass is scraped off after using. Make sure air vents are clean.

Changing mower blades
This is a chore that everyone hates. Cuts, bruises, skinned knuckles and other such injuries are common when mower blades are changed. These are not necessary, though, if the job is taken slowly and carefully, and the following precautions are taken:

- Disconnect the spark plug lead first to prevent the accidental starting of the mower. If the engine is a 4-stroke it is important, when you tip the mower on its side, that you keep the spark plug side uppermost, otherwise engine oil will get into the cylinder above the piston, making subsequent starting very difficult.

- Be careful setting the cutting height adjustment when mowing. If it is set too low the blades will be more easily damaged and require changing more often; also, the nuts holding the blades may become burred as they hit objects in the grass and the soil, making them harder to remove. As a general rule, replace nuts and washers each time blades are replaced.
- Make sure you fit and remove the blades according to the manufacturer's instructions.
- Use the correct blades.
- Keep the nuts and washers holding the blades well lubricated to prevent their seizing or rusting.
- Use ring spanners where possible; open-ended spanners slip more readily, especially when the holding nuts are partly burred. Use the correct size spanners.
- Don't over-tighten the holding nuts.

Lawn maintenance

Aeration

Aeration involves punching holes into a lawn to improve drainage, water penetration and root growth. In some cases aeration is also done to reduce thatch build up. Lawns on heavy soils, or which suffer a lot of use, need aerating regularly if the grass is to remain healthy. Aeration can be carried out manually (using a fork), or with a special aerating machine.

Coring the turf can be carried out manually using a tool similar to this, or by machines.

• Coring

Coring is one of the best ways to aerate. It involves removal of cores of soil using a hollow tine (i.e. metal tube) which plunges into the soil and extracts a core. This method leaves a clean hole in the turf without causing any further compaction at all. Coring equipment can be as simple as a hollow-tine fork (available from specialist garden shops) which is used manually in small areas, or quite complex self-propelled mechanical units.

After coring a turf, the cores of soil left lying on the surface must be swept or raked and removed from the lawn. Often a light topdressing is applied 7 to 14 days after coring a lawn. This will fill depressions left by the operation and help maintain levels.

• Spiking

Spiking doesn't work as well as coring, but anyone can 'spike' a lawn using just a common garden fork. Unlike coring, spiking does not entail removal of soil. Holes are made by simply pushing soil to the side as the tines of the garden fork penetrate. This method will create a compacted zone of soil around the edge of the hole it creates—for this reason spiking is nowhere near as effective as coring for aeration purposes. If the soil suffers too much compaction prior to spiking, this treatment might create holes surrounded by an even more compacted, impermeable layer of soil on their sides.

If there is an impermeable surface layer such as dry algae, spiking may be of advantage in breaking the surface to allow penetration of water and fertiliser, but generally, spiking is considered only a for this reason short-term answer to aeration problems.

Rolling lawns

Rolling is a technique used for flattening/levelling a lawn surface. It is particularly important on greens and other sporting surfaces where a perfectly level surface is critical. Frequent rolling will cause compaction, though, and unless aeration is also frequently used, it is not advisable.

Topdressing

Topdressing involves spreading a thin layer of specially selected soil over the top of existing turf. This might be done for any one of the following reasons:

Thatch control. Thatch is a tightly intermingled layer of dead vegetation and turf plants at soil level. As time goes on, leaves and roots die and are replaced by new growth, thus thatch is continually increasing. Topdressing places a thatch-free layer of fresh soil on the surface.

Levelling. Regular topdressing helps maintain an even surface to a lawn. Unless this or some other operation is carried out, a turf will become uneven (e.g. when someone stands on a wet lawn and they leave a depression, or when an insect burrows under the grass and its tunnel collapses).

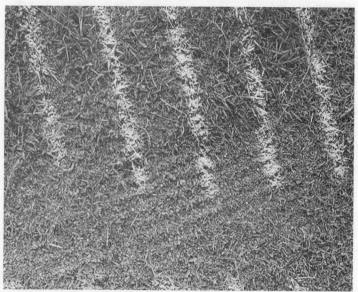

Topdressing is usually only done to correct unevenness in the lawn.

Revitalising. By adding fresh soil to a turf, soil structure may be improved (e.g. if sand is top dressed onto a clay soil). Fresh soil also introduces new nutrients to the turf.

Winter protection. In areas of extreme cold, a topdressing in late autumn can give winter protection to warm-season grasses such as couch.

Covering a sowing of seed, stolons or rhizomes. New nutrients are made available by the fresh soil.

Watering

Lawns need a lot of water during the drier months in order to maintain even growth. Water should to be applied to the lawn in an even distribution pattern, so that no dry patches are created.

A purpose-built irrigation scheme incorporated into the lawn will achieve the best results. Systems need not be complicated in design, and local hardware stores will usually have off-the-shelf kits available as well as a good supply of extra fittings etc. to help you build the perfect. Systems can either be incorporated into the lawn whilst it is under construction or they can be installed after the lawn is laid.

Pulsed watering

On heavy soils, watering every day often keeps the surface of the soil wet while the lower soil remains dry. If this happens, the roots of both grass and garden plants will tend to come to the surface. Pulsed watering is a way of getting the water to penetrate deeper and, by keeping a reservoir of moist soil deeper down, less watering becomes necessary. Simply, pulsed watering involves putting the sprinkler on for a short period, turning it off for 5–15 minutes to allow the water to soak in, then putting it on again for another short period. Repeating this procedure several times once every 3–4 days in even the hottest weather will use less water and result in a healthier lawn than watering heavily every day.

TREE CARE AND TREE SURGERY

Working as a tree surgeon is a very demanding job. It requires a high degree of physical fitness, alertness at all times, and attention to detail since much of a tree surgeon's job requires working at heights. Handling cutting tools and heavy weights in this situation is very risky unless the mind is kept sharp, the body healthy and you are always thinking one step ahead of what you are doing. Many groundwork operations are also potentially dangerous (e.g. felling, handling chainsaws, chemicals etc.).

There is no substitute for education and experience in tree surgery. If you are interested in starting a business, it is advisable to prepare. Formal education in Arboriculture and Tree Surgery is available at most local colleges (see Appendix). In addition to study, you should plan to work as part of a tree surgery gang prior to starting out on your own. Insurance and equipment costs can be quite high so, while the business may be very lucrative, there is a substantial start-up cost involved. A reputable tree surgeon will be a member of a professional association such as the Arboricultural Association or the Tree Surgeons Guild.

Some of the procedures involved in tree surgery are cavity work, where rotten wood is removed and the hole is filled, usually with concrete; thinning, when branches are removed to reduce the weight in the crown, thus reducing the likelihood of the tree (or branches) falling; bracing and cabling, to stop branches splitting apart. Most of these are specialist treatments and should be undertaken by experts only.

Tree surgery techniques

Cavity treatments

This procedure can be compared with cavity work dentists carry out on teeth that have developed rot in their tissue. It involves removal of rotten wood and filling the cavity with some solid material. Concrete is a very common and popular cavity filler, though polyurethane foam has also been used. (NB: For very large procedures, where the tree might need some structural strength in the cavity, concrete will provide this—foam won't.)

Cavities can start from neglected bark injuries or from a stub left after a branch has fallen or been removed. To minimise the necessity for cavity work, wounds should always be treated—clean with a sharp knife, cutting back to healthy tissue, then water and feed the tree to ensure it has ample vigour to combat any fungal attack on the exposed tissue.

Bracing and cabling

These techniques are aimed at holding branches together that are in danger of breaking and falling.

Bracing involves bolting metal rods into position between two branches to prevent them from splitting apart.

Cabling involves tying the branches together, using a metal cable attached to eye bolts that have been placed through the branches.

Propping

This technique is extensively used in Europe, but is rarely seen in Australia. Like cabling or bracing, propping is an operation carried out to prevent damage. It involves placing a wooden or metal prop between a branch and the ground to prevent the branch sagging and breaking.

Draining

Holes are drilled through wood in the bottom of a cavity to allow any water that collects inside it to drain out. By removing moisture from an area the likelihood of further wood rot is greatly reduced.

Bark wounds

Bark can be damaged in many different ways. Machinery such as mowers can bump or scrape it accidentally, animals or vandals may tear or bruise it, or gardeners might even damage it inadvertently with tools.

When the outer bark is removed, torn or crushed, the more vulnerable inner tissue of the tree loses its protection from infection and the threat of wood rot is considerably increased. The likelihood of infection, and the speed with which infection spreads, will vary from species to species. The best treatment is to try to avoid damage ever occurring. Any broken or bruised bark should be cut back to sound healthy wood as soon as damage is detected. This may be done using either a very sharp knife or (on large wounds) a sharp carpenter's chisel and a rubber mallet. The shape of the cut should, where possible, run in a line with the sap flow (up and down the trunk rather than across it), which gives a better chance of healing. Horizontal wounds are difficult to cut this way—all you can do is cut back to sound bark. If a horizontal wound is severe (e.g. ringbarking) you can sometimes help regrowth by grafting pieces of young shoots across the cut. This technique of 'bridge grafting' is often used in orchards to repair rabbit damage.

Feeding and watering a tree that has suffered a wound may help it to recover better. Regular checks on wounds (say every 6 to 12 months) are advisable. If the tree is calousing (i.e. regrowing) evenly right around the edge of the wound, this indicates good healing. When the wound is healing well on one side of the wound, but not so well on the other, cut further back into healthy tissue on the side not growing back well, then paint with a systemic fungicide. Another possibility is to do a bridging graft, but this requires someone with grafting expertise. If these alternatives do not work, there might not be a lot more that can be done.

The use of wound sealants on these areas has been debated in recent years. Many expert tree surgeons believe that tree wound paints have little more than cosmetic value (i.e. if the wound is painted, you will not notice it as much).

The two sides of the argument are that a) if you seal the wound, you stop infection getting to the damaged tissue, therefore wood rot is less likely and, on the other hand, b) if you use a wound sealant, you are sealing any infection in. The sealant will create a humid and warmer atmosphere underneath it, creating an atmosphere likely to promote a more rapid growth of infection.

Perhaps you should try both ways, and over a period of time make your own choice about whether to use or not use sealants.

Safety aspects

Tree surgery is potentially one of the most dangerous areas of horticultural work; however, proper training and adherence to basic principles of safety will greatly reduce the risk of accidents occurring.

There are four main aspects to safety in tree surgery: •Safety for the tree surgeon and his team •Safety to the public •Care of property/equipment •Implementing safety regulations.

Safety for the team

People working in tree surgery should always be fit! It is reasonable to insist that all persons involved in such work have regular medical checks. Obvious disabilities such as high blood pressure, heart problems or epilepsy will eliminate some from this type of work. Eyesight and hearing should also be perfect. Even a headcold can make for a more dangerous situation in a tree.

Alcohol and drugs. Staff who drink excessively or who take prescribed or non-prescribed drugs may be unsuitable for tree surgery work.

First Aid. Always keep a First Aid kit nearby when working in or felling trees. There should always be someone on site who knows how to use the kit and is trained in basic First Aid.

Accident procedures. There should be an established procedure for recording details of all accidents, whether they appear serious or not. Such records become important in the event of compensation claims.

Work teams. Tree surgeons should never work alone. Help must be within

Always wear protective clothing outdoors and use knee pads for protection.

calling distance. One man should always command an operation. It is safer for only one man to work in a tree at a time. Ideally there should be two others on the ground. The man in the tree should be given ample breaks from climbing. He must not be allowed to become fatigued at all. Ideally, two of the three-man team will take turns working in trees, with the third on the ground to support them.

Weather conditions. Do not attempt to work in trees in adverse conditions (e.g. if it is blowing a gale, if it is raining, or if frost has made the branches slippery.

Clothing

Footwear should be able to grip well (e.g. rubber soles), be strong, lightweight, comfortable and have waterproof uppers and built-in toe caps.

Trousers should be heavy (denim jeans have proven good) and not loose-fitting.

Body clothing: A shirt is essential, even in warm weather. Close-woven knitted jumpers may be needed in cold weather. These items should be tight-fitting.

Headwear: Safety helmets are not recommended for climbers but are essential for ground staff.

Gloves should only be used when handling dangerous chemicals (i.e. plastic gloves).

Goggles should be worn to protect the eyes from wood chips or other foreign bodies, particularly when using a saw.

Ear muffs are important when using loud machinery such as chain saws and chipping machines

Safety equipment for climbers

Even with the introduction of travel towers, there will always be the need for tree surgeons to climb. Towers simply can't get into all the places where work needs doing. The main items of equipment needed for climbing are:

Safety harness. Although there are many different types of harness available, most of them are designed for climbing power poles or forestry work. Few harnesses have been specially designed for tree surgery work. You are advised to speak to experienced tree surgeons about the pros and cons of what you propose to buy before making a purchase. A good harness can make the difference between life and death.

Ropes. A lifeline attached to the harness should be used at all times you are working in a tree. Most use 12 mm (½ inch) diameter rope as a lifeline. Nylon rope is not recommended because it can stretch, although some argue that nylon is better because of its elasticity. In any case, you should not use weakened ropes. The lifeline, in particular, should always be a relatively new rope. If a rope has experienced a great strain once, it should not be used again in a safety-critical situation.

Public safety

If working above roads, pedestrian walkways or anywhere where people might move near the work area, it is important to put up barriers and danger signs and restrict people from moving into the area. If you are burning any material removed from the tree, make sure that fire is permitted, and that it does not annoy anyone (some people may have washing out or be working in their backyard downwind of the fire). At no time should tools, particularly cutting tools, be left unattended. In operations involving the control of cars and pedestrians, additional staff will be necessary.

You should always be careful of buildings, power lines and other structures close to the trees you are working in. There are normally regulations governing how close one can work to power lines: become familiar with these. Do not attempt to drop branches from above a building unless you are experienced in controlling the fall.

Safety regulations

There can be numerous regulations relating to working in trees. Some of them you may be completely ignorant of ... you should make a point of *not* being ignorant.

- The employer may have regulations.
- Unions may have regulations.
- There may be a bonus scheme for dangerous work (the worker may be paid a higher rate when climbing).
- Discipline must not be breached in tree work. If a climber does not follow an order, this is very serious.

STARTING AN INDOOR PLANT SERVICE

Interior plantscaping is a much bigger business than many people realise. Offices, shopping centres and other commercial sites use indoor plants primarily for decoration, though there are other subtle benefits as well (e.g. plants will help purify and freshen the air). An interior plantscaping business may provide the following services:

Supplying indoor plants. This can include replacing indoor plants when they get sick or too large. Plants are sometimes sold to a client; alternatively, they may be hired.

Maintaining plants. This can involve routine visits to a premises, perhaps once or twice a week (or as required), to water, fertilise, prune off dead leaves, control pests and diseases, and perhaps wash or polish the foliage (foliage can gather dust, which should be washed off. Wiping or spraying with an appropriate oil can make the leaves glisten and look very attractive).

Moving plants. Plants may be moved or replaced periodically. Sick plants can be taken away, potted up, restored to health, and then returned. Plants may need to be moved to more appropriate positions in different seasons. An ideal position beside a window in winter, for example, might be too hot for a plant in summer

Interior landscaping. The same procedures can be applied here as are used for exterior landscaping. The only difference is that an interior landscaper needs to consider the special conditions that will influence the plants in the inside environment.

What to grow

Many plants can be grown as indoor plants, provided you give due consideration to their normal requirements and select cultivars that suit the conditions of the interior where they are to be placed.

Palms are popular indoor plants throughout the world, but many types of palms do not survive for long periods indoors, and must be rested in a greenhouse or out of doors relatively often.

The pygmy date palm (*Phoenix roebelinii*) is one palm that will withstand less light and more air conditioning than most other palms. This palm has the disadvantage of having sharp spikes, but in appropriate situations its hardiness to indoor conditions makes it a popular choice for interior plantscaping.

Indoor plant care

There are six main factors that need to be considered when growing plants indoors:

1. **Temperature.** Temperature fluctuations can result in plant stress, wilting and possibly death. Many plants have preferences for specific maximum and minimum temperatures—temperatures outside these limits will cause stress.

Sudden changes in temperature are frequently the result of heaters and air conditioners going on and off; doors opening and closing; and the use of cooking appliances.

2. **Light.** Plants have a specific requirement for light, both in terms of quantity and quality, and each plant's needs may be different. It is the knowledge and understanding of these individual plant requirements that makes for a successful interior plantscaper. Light can be too bright (e.g. near a window) or too dull. Lights being turned on and off, or being used for extensive periods can affect plants' physiological response (photoperiodism). Dust on leaves can block up leaf pores (stomata), and can also reduce the amount of light reaching the leaf itself. The light source itself (whether incandescent or fluorescent) will produce different light intensities, thereby affecting plant growth.

In office buildings, the task of the indoor plantscaper is to select suitable plants for low intensity fluorescent lights that will tolerate other environmental conditions such as air conditioning.

3. **Moisture.** Most indoor plants originated from understorey rainforest areas, hence they require an environment of medium to high humidity. Low humidity or dry air (particularly when heaters are being used) can cause plant stress. Air conditioners tend to reduce humidity down to 40–50%, which will provide a stressful environment.

Indoor plants will appreciate a light misting to increase the humidity around the plant. They will also benefit from a hosing down, if the plants can feasibly be removed form the office (or location), taken outside and hosed. This treatment is basically simulating a natural occurrence—rainfall. It will also wash dust off the leaves. Excessive moisture (as in over-watering) can be detrimental to the plant, causing root deterioration and possibly death.

4. **Nutrition.** All plants need nutrients to live, but in an indoor environment, where plant growth is often slow, care is needed in the amount used. The normal amount used for an outdoor plant could be considered excessive for the indoor plant. The easiest way for in indoor plantsperson to fertilise plants is either by slow release pellets (a practice that is carried out every few months) or liquid feeding (carried out almost every week)—depending upon product and season.

5. **Ventilation.** A lack of fresh air can be detrimental to many plants, particularly those with softer foliage. Many plants (such as *Radermachera* sp.) are known to release ethylene, which causes leaf drop; ventilation will help reduce this problem.

Gas from heaters or stoves can be toxic to many species, so keep plants away from these appliances. Cold draughts from an open window may also be a problem in some areas, even if the interior is generally warm. Still air and warm conditions may encourage problems like red spider mite and mealybugs.

6. **Growing conditions.** Plants in containers are growing under conditions that are very different from their natural habitat, therefore they need different treatment. Most plants can be grown successfully in a container, although some adapt much better than others. If plants are maintained properly you can try anything, provided you select the right size and type of container.

What is different about indoor plants?
- Drainage is better, so plants dry out more readily.
- The roots have a restricted area to grow in, so they can more rapidly become depleted of nutrients and water.
- The sides of the container can heat up and cool down, exposing the roots to more fluctuation in temperature than plants in the ground.
- The container itself can provide an eye-catching display or talking point.
- Vigorous plants can be kept separate from less vigorous varieties, so they do not compete with each other for nutrients.
- You can use tender plants that may not tolerate normal garden conditions.
- Plants can be moved into a prominent position while flowering or foliage is at an attractive stage, and replaced when out of season.

Choosing a container
Just about any container can be used for growing plants, provided it contains sufficient soil or potting mix for the plant to grow in, has suitable drainage, and does not contain or release any contaminants that may be harmful to plant growth. To get the best results, however, consider the following factors when choosing a container.
- Wide containers are less likely to tip over.
- Make sure the container has sufficient drainage holes to allow excess water to drain away quickly. Be careful also that the drainage holes are not too large, making it easy for potting mixes/soils to fall or wash out of the container.
- Choose the right size of container for the type of plant you wish to grow. A plant that will not grow very large will look out of place by itself in a large container, while a vigorous grower will soon outgrow a small container. In this case it is important to either re-pot regularly or choose larger containers to allow for such growth.
- In deeper pots the weight of the potting mix/soil will compress the material beneath it, reducing air spaces in the mix. A more open mix should therefore be used for deeper pots.
- Plant roots tend to coil more in round pots than they do in square ones. Root coiling is also reduced if the base is tapered.
- Most interior plantscapers use attractive outer pots (planters) then place the

indoor plant, still in its original plastic pot, within the planter. When the plant becomes jaded, they only need to lift the plant and plastic pot out and replace it with a healthy specimen. This way the attractive planter is constantly in use.

Caring for plants in containers

- Potting mixes in containers usually dry more rapidly than those in the ground because the container is more exposed to the elements—roots deep in the soil are insulated against fluctuations in temperature when the air heats up or cools down, but roots in a pot are still relatively close to the surface, hence susceptible to variations in temperature or dryness in the surrounding air. This means that greater care must be taken when watering plants in containers than for those in the ground. In the nursery, simple drip irrigation systems with individual drippers to each pot are a good way to overcome this problem.
- For plants that are placed in sunny positions, avoid dark-coloured pots that will absorb a lot of heat from sunlight. This can generate high temperatures in the potting mixture, which can severely damage plant roots. Light-coloured, glazed pots are good in such a situation as they will reflect a lot of the sunlight.
- Roots tend to grow through the bottom of containers when they are placed on top of something moist (e.g. if sitting in a saucer that is often wet). This can make them difficult to re-pot, and if the saucer does dry out a proportion of the roots can die, causing stress in the plant. This may be avoided by placing pieces of stone or tile in the saucer to lift the pot a little, then simply observing to ensure that the saucer does not get too wet or roots do not grow through too much.
- Sprinkling a layer of coarse sand over the soil surface in a container will reduce weed problems and control the growth of moss.
- For larger containers, mulches can be added to the potting mix surface to reduce water loss and to act as a buffer against dryness.
- When going away (e.g. on holiday) container plants might be moved for a period into a protected position out of direct sunlight and away from airconditioning and draughts. In the warm months containers might be placed in a trough, bath or similar container holding water, for a limited period (perhaps a few weeks). Take care not to immerse more than the bottom one-third of the container.

Potting up

How often you re-pot will vary considerably, depending on the type of plant you are growing, the conditions they are growing in, and the type of container they are growing in. Some plants, for example hoyas and some orchids, seem to flower best when they are somewhat rootbound. Most plants, however, do best when they are regularly re-potted into larger containers with fresh potting mix;

indeed, indoor plants do benefit from repotting every two to four years.

Plants that like to be pot-bound are better repotted into only slightly larger sized pots, whereas plants that dislike roots being disturbed are obviously best potted infrequently and into larger pots. Plants should be repotted if roots are filling a pot tightly (pot-bound) and are beginning to block up the drainage holes in the base of the pot.

How to pot up

Potting mix will compact over time, making watering more difficult, and both drainage and aeration poorer. Pot up plants as follows:

1. Before removing a plant from an old container for potting up, water it thoroughly. If the plant is dry it is best to immerse the old pot completely in a tub of water (a wet root ball will come out of an old pot far easier than a dry one).
2. If there is a tight mass of roots on the outside of the root ball, you should loosen those roots and break away 10–20% of the old potting mix before repotting. Remove a proportion of the top growth equal to the amount of root mass removed (i.e. if 20% of the roots are cut away, in most cases it is best to cut away 20% of the leaves, to reduce any stress on the plant).
3. Place some quality potting mix in the bottom of the new container.
4. Place the plant into the new container and fill around it with new potting mix. Firm the soil down lightly with your fingers. Do not fill the container to the top—leave at least a centimetre or more for watering.
5. Add slow release fertiliser to the top of the container, at a recommended rate.
6. Water thoroughly, then allow to drain.

Note: Watering with a weak seaweed fertiliser solution will help stimulate root growth and prevent any transplant shock

Potting mixes

Container plants are grown in a variety of media. Some are mainly a mixture of soils, others are a mixture that includes no soil at all. Some potting media are combinations of both soil and non-soil components.

The ideal potting medium should have the following attributes:

- Free of weed seeds.
- Free of pest or disease organisms.
- Freely draining and with good aeration.
- Able to retain sufficient nutrients and moisture for healthy plant growth.
- Waste salts from fertilisers should leach out of the soil easily.
- The mix should be heavy enough to make the pot stable, but light enough to minimise the effort involved in lifting the pot.

To make quality potting mix with uniform characteristics, very expensive screening and mixing equipment is required, hence the best mixes are expensive. Potting mixes can now be purchased carrying quality standard markings, such as the Australian Standards Logo.

Controlling pests

Be careful about spraying dangerous chemicals indoors. Pyrethrum or white oil are probably the safest insecticides and will kill most insects if you spray thoroughly (e.g. give a squirt from above, below and every side), as directed.

If you have to use dangerous pesticides, take the pot plant outside and treat it in a protected area out of the wind and the full sun; then bring it inside. Wash the area down afterwards to remove any concentrated residues on the ground. If there is an odour with the chemical, leave the plant in a well ventilated area prior to returning it to a closed room.

Weed control in pots

In established indoor plantscapes weeds are unlikely to emerge, but they may continue developing if they germinated prior to being placed into the site. Indoor plants usually have some type of surface mulching material (e.g. coconut fibre, hessian bags, peanut husks, etc.) primarily used for aesthetics to hide the pot and potting mixture.

When growing plants for indoor use, consider the following:
- Always use good quality potting mixes, free of weed seeds.
- Sprinkle a layer of coarse sand over the surface to stop the light reaching the moist potting mix below, and to make it easier to pull out the odd weeds which do germinate.
- Kill any weeds near pots before they (the weeds) produce flowers and seed (some weed varieties can produce over 10 000 new weeds from one old weed plant).
- There are weedicides available that nurserymen put on pots to kill weed seeds as they germinate. These are usually only available in commercial quantities from places such as stock agents and nursery suppliers.

Making life easier

Water-well pots

These pots have an extra container or well beneath the main container. This holds a reserve of water that can supply the plant for extended periods of several, or even more, weeks. The water is drawn up from the well by capillary action. The well is refilled through a hollow tube that reaches from the surface of the upper pot down into the well. Alternatively, there may be a reservoir entrance near the base to one side of the pot.

In some types clear plastic is used for the well section. This can sometimes lead to algal growth problems in the well. Air conditioning and draughty areas are good locations for water-well pots, as the plants use the water when they require it.

Water granules
When added to a potting mix, water granules help to increase its water-holding ability, thus reducing the frequency of watering. Water granules are generally clear and hard when dry, but when exposed to water they absorb large amounts of water, swell up, and take on a jelly-like appearance. If you use too many in a pot, they can swell and ooze out of the surface of the potting medium, becoming very unsightly.

Anti-transpirant solutions
These liquids are sprayed on plants for the purpose of slowing down their transpiration rate. In effect this reduces the amount of water required by the plant by those parts of the leaves which have been sprayed. New leaves, of course, will not have the spray covering and will therefor transpire at normal rates. The solution is only active for periods up to 3 months. Watering is still required after spraying—the benefit is that subsequent water consumption rate is lowered, reducing ongoing maintenance.

Dollies and other carts
A two-metre plant complete with clay pot and potting mixture can weigh a lot. Rather than risk back injury, use of dollies and other wheeled carts in your nursery saves labour and time. In some cases, front end loaders and hoists may also be necessary.

5
Gardening and Landscaping Tools

Maintenance of gardening tools and equipment can be a business in itself. Knowledge of how to maintain tools and servicing your own equipment can also be a great way to keep costs down for your gardening, nursery or landscaping business.

The way a tool is designed and built has a great effect on how well it can do a job. Consider the following:

- Strong tools will take greater physical stress and handle heavier jobs without breaking; if you buy a cheap tool built with cheap materials it might not last till the end of the first day, particularly if you are doing heavy work.
- Sharp tools put less stress on the tool, and less strain on you the user.
- Long handles give you greater leverage and increased reach, putting less strain on your back and other parts of your body.
- When you pay more for a tool, you are usually paying for long hours of thought that have gone into its design. Tools that do the job better and more easily are generally more expensive, but they could be well worth the additional outlay.
- If your soil is heavy clay or rocky, your tools are likely to be strained more— you will need better quality tools.
- If your soil is easy to dig (perhaps sandy), you may get away with using cheaper, poorer quality tools. Metal tools made with stainless steel or aluminium do not corrode like those made with other metals.

HAND SAWS
These have a variety of uses in the garden, ranging from pruning and lopping to construction of such features as fences and garden furniture. The most commonly used saws in the garden are:

Pruning saws. These generally have teeth designed to cut moist living timber and usually have teeth larger than those on saws used for cutting furniture or construction timber. There are two types of pruning saws:

straight blade which allows variation in the type of cut according to the type and size of the material being cut;

curved blade with teeth on one side. This curved saw is generally used by the experts because the curved blade allows access to restricted areas such as near closely interlocking branches.

Bow saws. As the name implies, these are bow-shaped. They are light-weight, easy to use, have replaceable blades, and coarse teeth which provide a fast cut when the blades are in good condition. This type of saw is popular for pruning branches that are too thick for light pruning saws.

Carpenter's saws. There is great variation in the types of saws used in carpentry work. Generally they have finer teeth compared to the pruning and bow saws, and these are generally set to give a narrower cut. This is because they are mainly used for cutting dried, milled, heat pressed and treated timber where a narrower, finer cut, in comparison to pruning cuts, is required. These saws are predominantly straight-edged with teeth on only one edge of the saw.

Simple rules for using hand saws

- Always keep the saw sharp. This makes cutting easier and gives a cleaner cut.
- Make sure you are only cutting timber. This applies particularly when cutting second-hand timber which may contain old nails, etc. and cutting in situations where the saw may come into contact with soils, gravels or other materials that are likely to damage the saw's cutting edge.
- Always store saws in a safe place and keep them clean. The saws may be readily damaged if dropped or banged against other materials. They will quickly rust if allowed to stay moist. Incorrectly stored saws may also present a safety risk, particularly if children and animals use the area.
- Use the right saw for the job at hand. This will make the task easier for you and produce a better quality job.

Snap-lock tools

There are several modular tool systems with a range of 'heads' that can be connected or disconnected to the one handle as required. Available heads include rakes, hoes and cultivators, aerators, seed sowers and pruners. Major advantages of this system are the space that is saved in storing tools and the flexibility of being able to vary the length of handle on a tool head.

The main disadvantage is that there is greater wear and tear on the handle and the locking mechanism than on any individual head.

Rakes

Rakes suffer a great amount of strain where the head meets the handle and, along with axes, are perhaps the tools most likely to suffer from broken handles. The prongs (or teeth) of a rake also suffer a great deal of strain, particularly if being used to create a new garden. If landscaping a new garden, get yourself the sturdiest rake you can find—or be prepared to go through several rakes before the job is finished.

Rakes may vary considerably in construction and in the type of materials used. The most common types of rakes include:

Grass and leaf rakes. These have long flat tines or teeth that lightly brush the surface you are raking, catching light loose material such as leaves and grass clippings. Some of the better quality rakes can be adjusted to change the width of the rake head to cater for differences in the size of the materials you are raking. These grass and leaf rakes are generally constructed of metal, bamboo, cane or plastic. The metal rakes generally last longer, but may rust unless they are plated. They are also usually more costly. The bamboo and plastic rakes don't have rust problems, and are generally cheaper than the metal ones, but are nowhere near as durable.

Nail rakes. Generally steel teeth are riveted to a steel frame. The teeth or tines are rigid and are shorter than the grass and leaf rakes. This enables shifting of heavier material and also gives the rake a cultivator-like effect on loose soils. If incorrectly used, the teeth may become loose.

Single piece rake heads. Generally formed from a single piece of carbon steel, sometimes from moulded plastic. This type has similar functions to the nail rake. Teeth size, shape and number vary according to the type of work to be undertaken. For example, you may have 10, 12, 14 or 16 teeth depending on whether you are raking fine or coarse gravel, asphalt or soil. Both nail and single piece rakes usually have sockets welded to the frame for the easy attachment of wooden handles.

Spades and shovels

Shovels are used for moving loose soil or other loose material. A shovel's blade is cupped and at an angle inwards from the line of the handle; it is not designed to dig.

Spades are used for digging and planting; the blade follows the same line as the handle. Spades and shovels can have short or long handles, with the blade curved (round mouth) or straight across the bottom (square mouth).

Long-handled spades provide greater leverage, placing less strain on the back, and give greater reach, allowing you to dig deeper holes. They are best suited for digging holes or trenches, particularly in hard clay soils.

Short-handled spades are better suited to use in confined spaces or for digging over established garden beds with relatively loose soil.

Forks

Forks are used to cultivate or mix soil, to aerate lawns (i.e. punch holes in a lawn to improve drainage or air penetration) or to move organic material about (e.g. turn over a compost heap). The prongs of a fork can be either round or flattened. Flattened prongs are more suitable for working with organic material.

Rollers

Rolling is a technique used for flattening/levelling a lawn surface. It is used to level new lawns prior to seeding, or to maintain a very even surface on established high-quality lawns. They are also used on gravel paths to compact and even out a loose surface, both during construction and periodically afterwards as part of ongoing maintenance. Sporting areas such as tennis courts are often rolled before they are played on, to remove any slight unevenness.

Rolling can damage lawns by causing compaction and developing drainage problems if frequent aeration is not carried out.

Rollers vary in size from small, light-weight models that are easily handled by one man, to large tractor-drawn models. It is unlikely that there would ever be the need to use anything but a lightweight roller in a home garden situation. It is best to avoid rolling lawns unless it is really necessary.

Rolling should be done when the surface is not too moist and preferably with relatively light-weight rollers. The weight of roller you use will depend on both the width of the roll and the soil type you are rolling. Heavier rollers are needed to make an impact on clay soils than are required on sands. Soils containing a high amount of organic matter will suffer less compaction than other soils.

Wheelbarrows

When buying a wheelbarrow, choose one that is solid and well constructed. Make sure the main centre of balance is over the wheel and not on your arms, and that you have plenty of leg room when wheeling the barrow. A well built wheelbarrow will last for several decades if properly maintained. Keep tyres pumped up, grease all moving parts, wash out soil or rubbish after use and store out of the weather. If these things are not done you will be lucky to keep a barrow in use for more than five years.

When using wheelbarrows the following simple rules should be followed:

- Don't overload—you will only damage the wheelbarrow, spill your load or hurt yourself.
- Use your knees when lifting the barrow—by keeping your back straight and bending your knees when lifting the handles of the wheelbarrow you will greatly reduce the risk of back damage.
- Have a clear working area—obstacles and uneven working surfaces put a strain on both you and the wheelbarrow, particularly as you try to balance your load.
- Use a rope when working on slopes—a partner pulling on a rope attached as low as possible at the front of the barrow will make getting up slopes a lot easier and much safer.

Sprayers

Sprayers are used for applying chemical sprays (insecticides, fungicides and weedicides), or liquid fertilisers. It is advisable to use a different sprayer for each type of chemical. (Note: Weedicide residues left from previous spray jobs can contaminate insecticides and damage plants you spray for insects.) Table 5.1 gives a comparison of costs, durability, etc. of the different types of sprayers available.

Disposable spray guns. Plastic bottles with a pump action handle on top. Many chemicals are sold as a ready-to-use spray in this type of bottle. Refills can be bought to screw on to the spray mechanism top. This type is OK for small jobs (e.g. spot spraying) but becomes expensive and time consuming for larger jobs.

Pressurised back or shoulder pack units. A container that can be pressurised with a flexible hose and connecting spray nozzle. The unit is pumped by hand to raise the pressure in the container. A trigger is used to release pressure and spray as required.

Motorised sprayers. The chemical is pumped from a container by a motorised pump, and out through a spray nozzle. This is suitable only for larger jobs.

TABLE 5.I. A COMPARISON OF SPRAYERS

	Disposable spray guns	Pressurised back packs	Motorised sprayers
Cost	Under $5	$50–$200	Most expensive
Durability	Use a few times only	Fair to good	Generally good
Parts	Not worth repairing	Parts available, can be repaired	Nozzle blockage Engine problems

Sprayer problems

Sprayer nozzles often get clogged with insects, bits of plants or other unwanted material. Pump wear and deterioration is brought about by ordinary use, but accelerated by misuse. The following suggestions will help minimise labour problems and prolong the useful life of the pump and sprayer.

Use clean water. Use water that looks clean enough to drink. A small amount of silt or sand particles can rapidly wear pumps and other parts of the sprayer system. Mains water or water pumped directly from a well is best. Water pumped from ponds or stock tanks should be filtered before filling the tank.

Keep screens in place. A sprayer system usually has screens in three places: a coarse screen on the suction hose, a medium screen between the pump and the boom, and a fine screen in the nozzle. The nozzle screen should be fine enough to filter particles that will plug the tip orifice.

Use chemicals suitable for the equipment. Some chemicals, such as liquid fertilisers, are corrosive to copper, bronze, ordinary steel, and galvanised surfaces. If the pump is made from one of these materials it may be completely ruined by just one application of liquid fertiliser. Stainless steel is not adversely affected by liquid fertilisers, and pumps made from this substance should be used for applying these types of treatments.

Don't clean nozzles with a metal object. To clean, remove the tips and screens and clean them in water or a detergent solution using a soft brush. The orifice in a nozzle tip is a precision machine opening. Cleaning with a pin, knife or other metallic object can completely change the spray pattern and capacity of the tip.

Flush sprayers before using them. New sprayers may contain large amounts of metallic chips and dirt from the manufacturing process. Sprayers that have been idle for a while may contain bits of rust and dirt. Remove the nozzles and flush the sprayer with clean water. Clean all screens and nozzles thoroughly before using the sprayer.

Clean sprayer thoroughly after use. After each day's use, thoroughly flush the sprayer with water, inside and out, to prevent corrosion and accumulation of chemicals. Be sure to discharge cleaning water where it will not contaminate water supplies, streams, crops, or other plants, and where puddles will not be accessible to children, pets, livestock or wildlife.

Power tools

Power tools make life much easier, but they are expensive to buy and potentially dangerous to use. If used and maintained properly power tools can last for decades, but be prepared to spend some of the time you save by using a 'motor' in maintaining that motor. Most power tools have parts that wear and need replacing from time to time. Moving parts wear out, but if kept clean and oiled and greased, the rate of wear is minimised. Corrosion is another major problem that can be greatly reduced by simply keeping metal parts clean and coated with oil.

Whenever buying power tools, (whatever the type of tool) consider the following:

- What size engine is it (compared with the competition)?
- Is it an established, well known product, and will parts be easily available?
- How easily can the salesman start the engine?
- How solid are the parts of the machine? (Is the body made of cheap plastic, cast iron, stainless steel or what?)
- What sort of guarantee is given, and what does the guarantee cover? (Good tools have a long-term, extensive guarantee)
- Are there any scratches, is there any corrosion, etc. on the machine? (Be sure you are not being sold a problem machine returned by another customer, or old stock that has been sitting about and is unsaleable).
- Try to find someone who has used the same model and was happy with it.
- Check the amount of vibration, and the strength needed to operate the machine. Are you comfortable using it, or will you find it too difficult to use?

Power tools are driven either by electricity or a petrol motor. Each type has its advantages and its shortcomings.

Electric tools
The main advantages are that these are generally cheaper to buy and more reliable to start. Major disadvantages are that many electric motors are not very durable and are harder to repair if they break down. It is also potentially dangerous to be dragging an electric cord behind you when using a power tool.

Safety with Electricity

- Don't let wires become exposed through insulated coverings
- Don't allow any parts of cables, plugs or electric machines to become loose.
- Don't overload a circuit by putting too many double adaptors on the one plug.
- Never use electric tools in wet conditions (e.g. an electric drill outside in light rain).
- Never use electric tools when a lightning storm is threatening.
- Don't pull the plug out by the cord—this can weaken the connections.
- Don't let water (or wet hands) get near any electrical cord.
- Don't switch on a power tool when it is partly dismantled.
- Always switch the power off before disconnecting a power tool.
- Don't work around live wires (e.g. lines connecting power to a building).

Remember, electricity can kill!

Petrol motor tools
The 'all thumbs', unskilled handyman frequently finds a petrol motor difficult to start. If you're in that category, don't give up. If you take time to listen to a mechanic and learn what you are doing wrong, you should be able to greatly improve your ability to start a petrol motor, and even undertake some of the basic repairs that are commonly needed. Once you learn how to set the choke, how to avoid flooding the engine, and how to clean a dirty spark plug, you should have eliminated a large slice of the troubles people usually face.

TABLE 5.2. COMMON PROBLEMS WITH PETROL ENGINES

Problem	Possible causes	What to do
Engine runs roughly	Water in fuel	Drain fuel, wash fuel tank and lines and refill
	Dirty spark plugs	Remove and clean off carbon
	Carburettor badly adjusted	Needs workshop service
	Ignition wire broken	Check wire to spark plugs, repair if necessary
Engine doesn't start	No fuel in tank	Check fuel level by dipping a very clean stick into tank if empty, fill up
	Fuel line tap turned off	Check, and open if necessary
	Clogged fuel line	Disconnect and wash clean with petrol
	Carburettor flooded	Leave for 5 minutes, then try again
	Dirty spark plugs	Remove and clean
	Wide spark plug gap	Remove plug and squeeze points together
Exhaust smoky	Wrong type of fuel	Get new fuel from a reputable mower shop
	Worn engine parts	Needs workshop repairs
	Timing wrong	Needs workshop service

Dirty spark plugs are perhaps the most common reason for a two-stroke engine (found on most mowers) not starting, or running roughly. This problem is easily fixed by removing the plugs with a socket spanner and cleaning off the soot (carbon) that has built up inside, using a sharp pin and a piece of fine sandpaper.

Chainsaws

Training is necessary before using a chainsaw. Most places that supply chainsaws will also provide excellent instruction on their use. These tools are virtually essential for large trees and branches, but can be extremely dangerous if the operator is uneducated in their use. Most chainsaws are powered by a two-stroke engine. Before buying and using a chainsaw you should be familiar with safety devices such as rear handle guard, chain catcher, anti-vibration system and safety lock-out switch. Wear eye goggles, ear mufflers and other protective gear when using chainsaws.

Starting a chainsaw

1. Check the fuel and chain oil.
2. Put the saw on the ground, making sure that the chain cannot get caught in scrub or branches.
3. Check that you know where all the controls are located.
4. Set the choke and throttle. Put your foot right through the rear handle; hold the front handlebar with your left hand.
5. Pull to feel if the starter mechanism is engaged.
6. Make a short sharp pull and follow through back with the starter handle.

As soon as the saw starts, check that it is pumping oil to the chain. Point the guide bar towards a stump or another light background with the chain running. You can then see whether chain oil is splattering out from the guide bar.

Sharpening the chain

The chain must be sharpened at regular intervals. Make sure that you have a few round files of the right size before using the saw. A distinction is made between touch-up filing and refiling. You can touch-up file the saw yourself. Follow the angle of the cutting teeth with the round file, and file carefully. Refiling should be entrusted to an expert. A vice and a few other accessories are needed to refile the chain. The exact filing angle for the type of chain in question must also be known. Chain refiling may be combined with the annual overhaul of the chainsaw.

Extending chain life

Chainsaw chains can wear out very easily if misused, and they're not cheap to replace. To get the most out of your saw, the following points should be observed:

1. Don't use the saw in dirty or gritty situations.
2. Avoid cutting timbers that might have nails or other foreign matter embedded in it (e.g. railway sleepers or used building materials).
3. Don't use a chain when it starts to become blunt. Depending on the conditions, you might need to sharpen the chain after only a dozen or so cuts.
4. Keep the chain properly tensioned (don't use it when it becomes loose).
5. Don't use an over-worn sprocket. A worn-out sprocket can destroy a new chain in less than a few hours.
6. Always use plenty of oil and never allow the oil to run dry.
7. Stop cutting immediately if the cut becomes crooked, and start afresh.

Brushcutters

Brushcutters are mainly used to cut long grass, or trim weeds and grass along fencelines, around the base of solid obstacles (trees, statues, seats, etc), or over

Rotary hoes can help produce new garden beds and aerate existing gardens quickly and efficiently. These machines can be purchased or hired.

Powered hedging clippers reduce time required to carry out maintenance.

ground too rough for a mower. There are two different types of brushcutters: those with a nylon cord that will cut grass and light weed growth, and those with a metal blade (like a circular saw), used to cut heavier growth such as woody weeds or scrub. A few simple safety rules should always be followed with either type:

1. Always wear goggles when using a brushcutter.
2. Never operate a machine close to other people (grass, twigs or stones can be flung at people).
3. Always wear thick boots and long pants.
4. Keep your distance from the spinning cord or blade and turn the machine off before putting it down.
5. Don't operate the machine when you are fatigued.

Nylon cord cutters (e.g. whipper snippers)
- A spinning nylon cord (up to 30 cm long).
- These are generally smaller, more lightweight and used for trimming around the edge of lawns, the base of buildings or trees, or cutting grass on slopes or other inaccessible places.
- These can be relatively cheap machines. The nylon cord is cheap and easy to replace when damaged.
- May be powered by an electric motor or petrol engine.

Metal blade cutters
- A spinning disc with blades made from plastic or metal.
- These are generally more heavy duty machines able to cut long grass, blackberries or, in the case of the more powerful machines, more substantial brush.
- The machines and blades are more expensive than the nylon cord brushcutters. The blades need to be kept sharp.
- Powered by petrol motors.

Many of these machines can be used as both whipper snippers or brushcutters, having scope for different heads (fittings).

Rotary hoes
Rotary hoes are used to loosen or cultivate soil, making it easier to dig in or move about. They may be self-propelled or driven by a PTO attachment to a tractor or mini-tractor. Self-propelled machines normally use petrol engines and move forward by rubber-tyred drive wheels or by using the rotating blades to pull the machine. Most need a reasonably strong and fit person to operate them properly.

Tractor-mounted machines are easier to operate but more expensive to buy (given that you need a tractor to operate them). Small self-propelled units are best in small areas and soil depths of 15 to 20 cm, while the tractor-operated versions are best for larger areas and where greater depths of cultivation are required.

A rotary hoe (with or without operator) can be hired at a very reasonable rate to cultivate soil prior to landscaping a new garden. The home gardener would not normally buy a rotary hoe unless it was going to be used regularly (perhaps to cultivate a large vegetable garden), whereas a full-time gardener or landscaper might have sufficient use for such a machine to warrant purchasing one.

Hedge trimmers

These involve two cutting blades that are moved backwards and forwards (reciprocated) in a scissor-like action to cut or trim shrubs or hedges. These blades may be powered by petrol-driven engines, by compressed air, or by electricity (either battery or mains power). The blades don't have the razor sharp edges that are found on pruners, but they have to be clean and undamaged, with cutting angles of just under 90° to achieve a clean, sharp cut.

TOOL MAINTENANCE

Looking after your tools is very important—well cared for tools don't have to be replaced as frequently. Tools in good condition are easier to use; they are also generally safer. Some simple reminders are listed below:

Metal. To prevent rust or corrosion, metal either needs painting with a good metal primer, or regular coating with oil (after using, clean and wipe metal parts with an oily rag).

Sharpening. Keeping your tools sharp usually means less effort is required to use them, so less strain is applied.

Washing. If tools are kept clean they are less likely to corrode or have moving parts seize. This also reduces the likelihood of spreading pests and diseases from infected areas to uninfected areas.

Storing. Keeping your tools stored properly means they are less likely to be damaged, lost or stolen. Tools left lying around can also be dangerous, particularly if there are young children about; they can also be used by burglars to break into the house, garage, sheds etc.

Oil

Oil is used to protect engines in four ways:

Lubrication. It must lubricate precision, low clearance parts in order to minimise friction and wear.

Cooling. It acts as a coolant to keep piston, connecting rod, and bearings all at safe working temperatures. This is especially important on air-cooled engines as there is no water jacket to help cool moving parts.

Sealing. It serves as a seal between cylinder walls and piston rings to ensure proper compression and prevent exhaust gasses from entering the crank case.

Cleaning. It acts as a cleaning agent to keep in suspension soot and varnish formed as a by-product of combustion. When the oil is drained, these agents are removed from the engine. In order to adequately protect an air-cooled engine it is important to select a high-quality lubricant that has been fortified with detergents and oxidation inhibitors.

About one gallon of water is produced for every gallon of fuel that is burned. When an engine is operating 'up to temperature', most of the water escapes harmlessly with the exhaust gases. When the engine is cold, however, some of the steam condenses on the cold cylinder wall, and works its way into the crankcase. Here it joins partly burned fuel particles and products of oil and fuel oxidation to form acids and sludge. Although this condition occurs more frequently in cooler climates, it can be a year-round problem when the engine is used only intermittently. High temperatures, on the other hand, promote oxidation of the oil, just as grease left on a hot barbecue will smoke and char. This oil oxidation forms a varnish-like deposit, the main cause of sticking rings and intake valves. It also produces a sludge that impairs normal lubrication.

Power tool maintenance

Always read the manuals or leaflets supplied with tools: there may be a regular servicing or maintenance procedure required. When instructions are not supplied, then a number of simple maintenance tasks will generally help prolong the life of power tools.

1. Check that all parts of the tool are free of foreign matter or obstructions that may impede the efficient, safe use of that tool.
2. Make sure that worn or damaged parts are replaced promptly.
3. See that all moving parts are well lubricated.
4. Protect (paint or wipe with an oily rag) any parts that are likely to rust or become corroded.
5. Keep battery terminals free of corrosion and battery levels topped up. All connections should be kept tight.
6. Make sure any oils are kept topped up, and drained and replaced at regular intervals.
7. Keep air cleaners clean and unblocked.
8. Keep any cutting edges properly sharpened.
9. Periodically check for and tighten any loose nuts, bolts, screws etc.

6
Landscaping

There are two areas of landscaping services that you might consider. One is to design, the other to build or construct. Some landscapers do both, others might even specialise in just one aspect or style of design or of construction. Some of the options for specialisation are:

- Small or courtyard gardens
- Permaculture designs
- Formal gardens
- Budget-price gardens
- Natural gardens

Some designers or contractors distinguish their service by concentrating on a particular type of feature, or a particular type of plant. Options might be:

- Rose gardens
- Paving
- Timber structures (e.g. gazebos, pergolas)
- Native plants
- Water gardens
- Ferneries
- Paved areas

Development of a native garden is simple—just try to mimic nature.

If you can develop a unique skill or feature to offer clients, you may be able to create a very strong niche market. Statuary and trompe l'oeil (trick-of-the-eye effects) are just two such features. Certain landscapers are in high demand because, when they do a job, the client can get a 'work of art' such as this as part of the package.

A garden design service can be offered in the following ways:

1. A consultation only	Visit, give verbal advice, and no more.
2. A concept plan	A plan drawn to scale but lacking detail—only providing a broad concept.
3. Garden design	A plan drawn to detail, showing planting details, specifying other features and components but not specifying the construction detail of hard* landscaping (e.g. the plan may indicate the location of a wall and say it is to be built with stone, but it won't specify foundations, drainage etc. to be incorporated into the wall).
4. Full landscape plans and specifications	These contain full and fine detail, including construction details of structures (e.g. a plan of how to build a wall, showing drainage, foundations, etc.

* Hard landscaping refers to items such as walls, paths, pergolas, rock work, concrete pond construction, etc. Soft landscaping involves the lawns and plants.

STARTING A GARDEN DESIGN SERVICE

Designing a garden takes artistic flair combined with good knowledge of available materials and a practical, systematic approach. These skills are something that need to be learnt properly if you are to succeed in applying them in a business.

Often people develop a wonderful home garden for themselves, and are subsequently encouraged by friends to 'go into landscaping'. If this describes you, then you probably have potential to become a successful landscaper, but you will still need at least some basic training. Running a garden design business, making money out of it, and keeping customers satisfied, is different from developing a couple of home gardens that satisfy yourself and your friends.

A necessary characteristic for a garden designer is the capacity to compromise. That doesn't mean you should not negotiate with your client to convince him/her of the merits of your plan, but if you can't gracefully accept another's (the client's) point of view and ultimate decision, then it may be difficult for you to achieve the word-of-mouth recommendations that are the lifeblood of the landscape designer's business.

An example of the sort of compromise that often occurs is given in Figures

Above: *A difficult site needing landscape work.*

Left: *A few days later with planting completed. Note the spaces between plants to allow for their growth, and that paths do not need to be straight.*

6.1 a. and b.: Although the gravel paths and drive give an aesthetically pleasing 'flow' to the Concept Plan (a), the final detailed Garden Design (b) shows that the client opted for a paved drive, probably because it would better stand up to the traffic on it—and he probably vetoed the pergola over the front gate to compensate for the extra cost of the paved drive.

When you start

- Only take on small jobs at first (e.g. courtyards or parts of larger gardens).
- Take photos of jobs you do, to show clients in the future.
- Collect books and magazines with photos of gardens which you can discuss with clients (but only show them things that you are confident about designing and/or building).
- As you do designs, make copies for yourself, and put together a folio of plans that you can show potential clients.

DESIGNING A GARDEN

Planning is the first step towards a successful garden. This is much easier if you are developing a new garden from scratch, because you don't have the problem of choosing what parts of the old garden will be scrapped. If renovating an existing garden, be ruthless! Don't hesitate to change the shape of paths and garden beds or rip up lawn areas completely. You will, however, paint the best picture on a clean canvas.

The best-planned gardens are tackled the same way: systematically, step by step, by drawing ideas on paper then taking time to reflect and review those ideas, before starting any construction. Garden design experts suggest different steps to follow and all are valid, as long as you take time to consider what you are doing before spending time and money on any garden construction. A typical planning process follows.

1. Consult with the client

In designing a garden it is of paramount importance to identify the needs and desires of the client and to produce a concept that, within the bounds of money and environment, meets those requirements. It is at this early stage that well developed listening skills will be extremely useful, as well as the tact and diplomacy to point out where the client might be asking for the impossible (e.g. tropical plants in Tasmania, or large expanses of paving that the budget cannot afford).

Questions that may help you at this stage include: Does the client want a low-maintenance garden? Does he/she have particular preferences or dislikes in plants? Will the yard need to cope with children who like to kick a ball around? Is the garden to be primarily functional and/or aesthetic? Does the client enjoy outdoor entertaining? Is a herb garden on the wish-list? The information gleaned

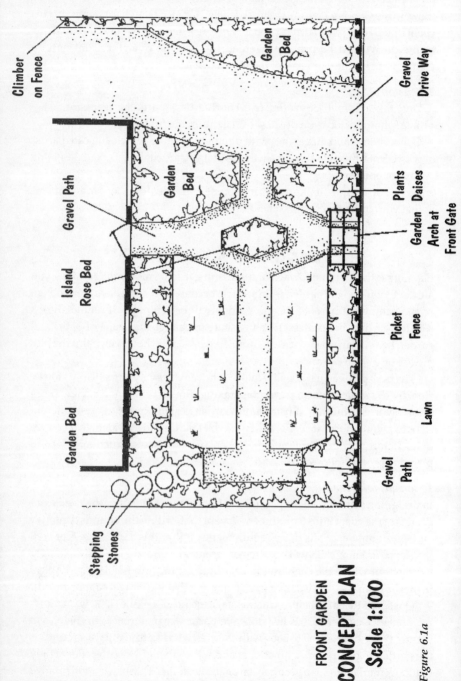

Climber on Fence

Garden Bed

Gravel Drive Way

Gravel Path

Garden Bed

Plants Daises

Island Rose Bed

Garden Arch at Front Gate

Garden Bed

Picket Fence

Lawn

Gravel Path

Stepping Stones

FRONT GARDEN
CONCEPT PLAN
Scale 1:100

Figure 6.1a

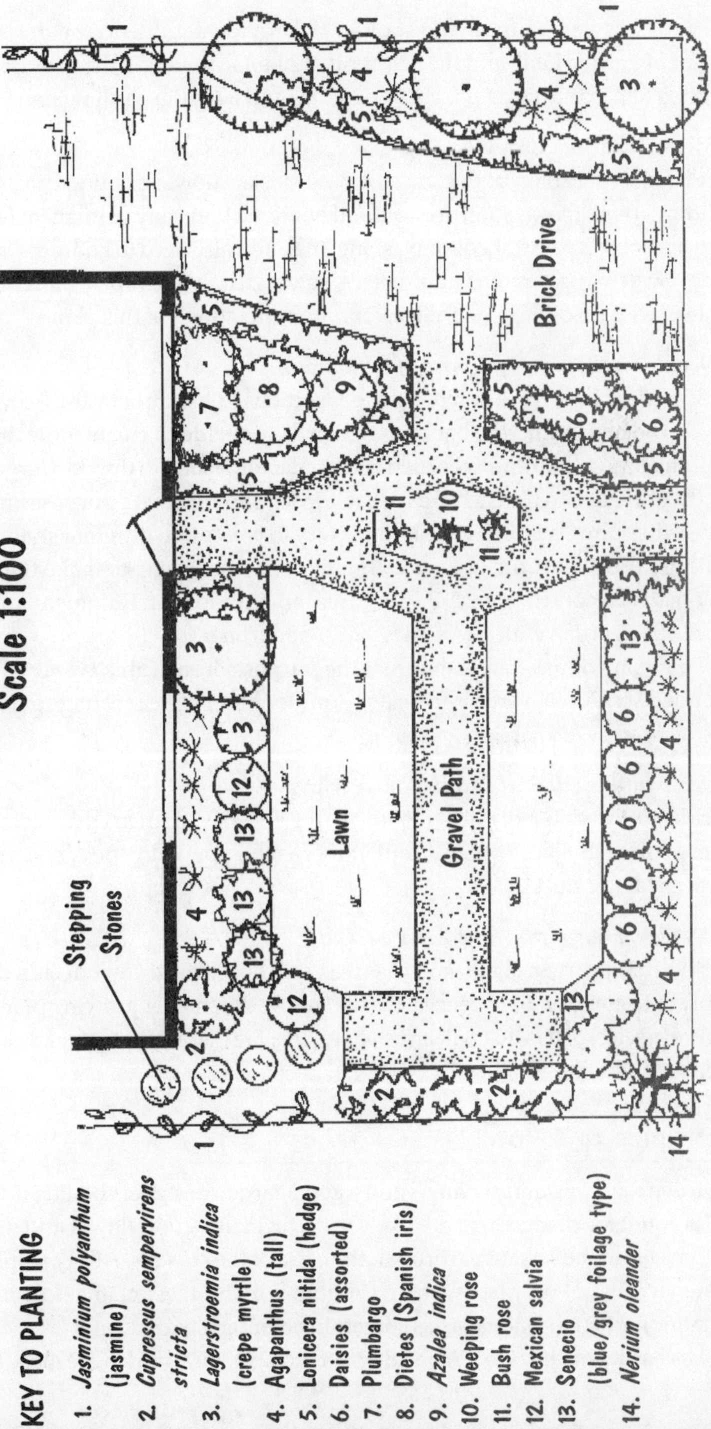

GARDEN DESIGN
Scale 1:100

KEY TO PLANTING

1. *Jasminium polyanthum* (jasmine)
2. *Capressus sempervirens stricta*
3. *Lagerstroemia indica* (crepe myrtle)
4. *Agapanthus* (tall)
5. *Lonicera nitida* (hedge)
6. Daisies (assorted)
7. Plumbargo
8. *Dietes* (Spanish iris)
9. *Azalea indica*
10. Weeping rose
11. Bush rose
12. Mexican salvia
13. *Senecio* (blue/grey foilage type)
14. *Nerium oleander*

Stepping Stones

Lawn

Gravel Path

Brick Drive

Figure 6.1b

from the answers to these questions will provide a guide to the design and layout of garden beds and the selection of plants, as well as the provision and location of hard surfaces, gazebos/pergolas and even the washing line.

2. Measure up and draw the area

You need a basic plan of the site as it now exists, showing boundaries, fences, buildings (with the position of doors and windows), and any permanent features such as concrete paths, sheds or washing lines. You also need to know the location of any water or gas mains and meters, sewers, drainage pipes, underground cables, etc. If possible, make at least three or four copies of this plan.

3. Decide on the broad purpose of each area

Most gardens have three or more obvious sections (e.g. the front yard, a courtyard beside the house, and the backyard). You may decide to create more areas by building fences, planting a garden bed or placing a shed to divide a larger area into two smaller areas. Each area of the garden should have a purpose and may have a different style, but you shouldn't try to create two different styles in the same area. The purpose of an area might be aesthetic (e.g. to make the house look better) or practical (e.g. a work area, an outdoor entertainment area or a productive garden with vegetables, herbs and fruit).

Draw on your sketch plans what the purpose of each area is and what the intended style of that area is to be (e.g. 'outdoor living area/cottage garden' or 'aesthetic area/formal rose garden').

4. Draw in the physical details for each area

Decide on the shape of garden beds, paths and paved areas, then determine where you might locate, for example, any gazebos, pergolas, ponds, statues, or other garden features.

5. Decide on the plants for each area

Start with the larger plants such as trees and tall shrubs. Next decide on any climbers to cover walls or fences. Lastly, choose the smaller growing plants and be sure to select plants that will grow well alongside the larger plants and climbers already selected.

Principles to follow

A garden will constantly change, and a good garden designer should anticipate and account for changes that are likely to occur. Plants grow, flower and die. The garden continually changes through the cycle of the seasons. An accomplished gardener will not only be aware of this, but will use these changes to create a dynamic garden that always has something of interest in it.

The basic principles to be considered as you design a garden are those things

Concept Plan for Home Garden with Formal Front Garden

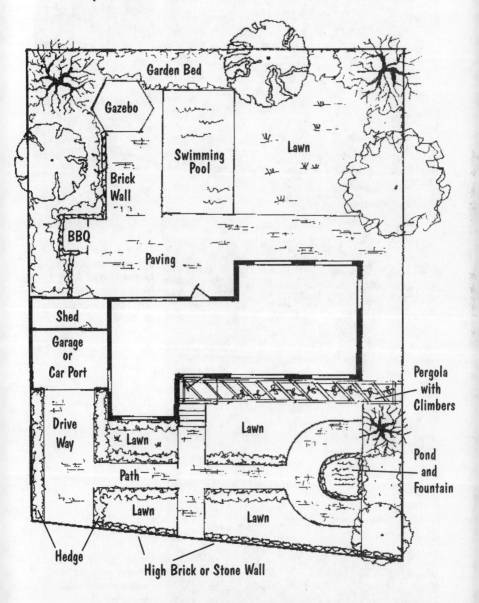

Figure 6.2. *Landscape designer's Concept Plan for leisure garden and formal front garden for a business couple who like outdoor entertaining.*

Large paved flat areas are more used than turfed sloped land. Notice the mild terracing to overcome the slope.

Ensure water features such as creeks, ponds and fountains are watertight and long-lasting.

that influence the way in which the components (e.g. plants, structures or paths) are arranged. If you can grasp an understanding of the following 'principles', that will go a long way towards helping you create a truly stunning garden:

Unity. A repetitive pattern (e.g. an avenue of standard roses) can be used to create unity. A lawn, a path, mass planting of one species, or water flowing through a garden can be used to tie other components of the garden into one cohesive unit.

Balance. This refers to an equilibrium, either symmetrical (duplication on either side of an imaginary line) or asymmetrical (dissimilar placement of different objects or masses on either side of the same type of imaginary line, but in a way that an equilibrium exists).

Proportion. This refers to proper sizing or scaling of components in relation to each other; for example, a 30 m tall eucalypt would look out of place in a small courtyard garden.

Harmony. This is usually the prime objective of any landscaper, so that different parts of the landscape fit together.

Contrast. Contrast is in opposition to harmony and should not be overdone, otherwise chaos may result. Occasional contrasts to the harmony of a design will create an eye-catching feature in a garden, adding life and interest to an area that would otherwise be dull.

Rhythm. Rhythm is a conscious repetition of equal or similar components in the garden. It is usually created by repetition and transition.

Formal or informal?

Formal gardens are orderly, often with symmetry in their design and a highly manicured appearance. The pathways and garden beds are frequently arranged on either side of a central pathway in regular shapes. Each side of the path is a mirror image of the other side.

Informal gardens are not symmetrical; they can be more natural in appearance and an untidy appearance often does not look out of order. Straight edges to garden beds or pathways will create a more formal effect, while curved edges create a more informal and relaxed feeling.

Formality in a garden is not a black and white thing, though. There is an unlimited range of compromises between the very formal and totally informal garden.

Develop a garden in stages

Often the garden has to be developed in stages because of the amount of money or preparatory work required. When preparing a plan take this into consideration—perhaps preparing detailed plans only for the areas that are to be developed fairly quickly, and simply designating broad ideas for future development on a larger plan of the area.

If large areas will be undeveloped for substantial lengths of time, then consider screening with fast-growing plants or a temporary fence until that area can be attended to. Areas designated for paving, garden beds or water gardens might be mulched to provide a reasonable appearance until work commences. The mulch can be used in other parts of the garden to enrich the soil when the development occurs. Pot plants filled with colourful annuals, perennial or groundcovers can make the outdoor area attractive even while it is still under construction. The plants can be used in the garden beds later.

Hold out for quality

If money is a problem, cut costs but not quality.

There are two types of costs involved in a garden: the first cost is building it, the second is maintaining it. Often if a little more time, effort and money is spent on building the garden, then the cost of maintaining it can be greatly reduced. Gardens that are initially cheap to build tend to require ongoing repair and

Landscaping either for private gardens or public spaces is the same—quality of workmanship is very important.

Intricate construction design with rocks, pebbles, wood and plants—but also high maintenance.

A barrier surrounding landscape work areas is a safety precaution all sites should instigate.

maintenance of the hard materials used. This type of problem can, however, be largely avoided by using good quality materials, and they are not necessarily more expensive ones.

Creating a garden with limited money is not difficult, but it may require some compromises. Here are a few alternatives you could discuss with your clients.

TABLE 6.1. MAKING COST-CUTTING CHOICES

Material	Cheaper alternative	Comments
Concrete paths	Asphalt paths	Not quite as permanent
	Gravel paths	Weeds can grow; not always good in the wet.
	Stepping stones	Difficult with prams, etc.
	Sleepers	Will rot, can be dangerous.
Pergolas for shade	Trees	Can drop leaves; the wrong types can have damaging roots; slow to establish
Irrigation systems	Mulch Use drought-tolerant plants	Choice of plants restricted
Stone retaining walls	Recycled rubber tyres, tree trunks/branches	Can look ugly, at least until plants can be grown over them. Might not be able to cut into slope as much.
Fences	Wire mesh with creepers	Slow to establish, need to be cared for
Stone or ceramic garden ornaments	Concrete copies	Not as attractive
Large ceramic pots	Plastic pots or large recycled containers (tubs, barrels, etc.) Concrete copies	Not as attractive
Colorbond pool fence	Timber picket or paling fence	Might not look as good; might have splinters

7

Starting a Landscape Construction Service

Landscape construction covers many different areas. Some construction companies will choose to do all aspects of landscaping, including installing plants, paved areas, decks, water features and any other outdoor feature. Other companies will elect to specialise, such as installing fences only, or only doing plant and lawn installations and leaving the 'hard' features to another firm. Regardless of which road you choose to go, either specialist or full service, there are some criteria necessary for success in landscape construction.

First of all, a willingness to undertake hard work is essential. Planting trees and constructing features means digging into all types of soils, from nice loams to hard clay or rocky substances. The successful contractor must also be tolerant of all types of weather, as well as being sensible about the weather. It is nice to think of working out of doors on a sunny spring day, but working outside in the

Laying down lawn is a more common practice in landscape jobs than sowing seeds.

heat of summer or on a cold, wet winter day can be very uncomfortable. Working in the heat, especially in very hot areas, can also be a health risk and may sometimes necessitate a shorter working day.

A lot of landscape construction work can be made easier with the use of mechanical equipment. Hiring equipment is an ideal way to get started in the business without having to outlay money for expensive pieces. However, once business is established, purchasing equipment may be more cost effective. A trailer or utility vehicle for hauling materials is often needed, too.

As with all areas of business, the key to a happy customer is to make it clear exactly what service is being provided. Client perception is often different to a contractor's perception and it is not uncommon for this to lead to disputes. You need to be a very good communicator, and make sure your client is clear on what they will be receiving for their money. Having agreements in writing and backing up any discussions with drawings of what the finished product will be and how it may look a couple of years later, is important. And while all businesses want to satisfy the customer, there is a duty, as a landscape contractor, to advise clients of what may become problems. For instance, a client may insist on a particular type of tree, but may not be aware of the size of the mature plant or how the root system may affect nearby structures or watercourses.

All this said, landscape contracting, while very hard, is very rewarding work. It is one of the areas where a hard day's labour can give instant results. And, as we move toward a more service-based society, less people have time to do their own landscaping and construction so the demand for landscape contractors will continue to increase.

Bobcats are best driven by an experienced operator.

SOILS AND LANDSCAPING

Regardless of whether you are building solid structures or installing plantings, you will be working with the soil. One of the most important factors in creating a successful landscape is understanding and properly managing the different soils that you will be working with. Soils usually form the foundation on which landscape features are formed, e.g. raised garden beds, mounds, ponds, lawns, as well as providing a base for paths and driveways. Soils also provide sustenance and support for plants in the landscape.

Earth forming

Slopes, mounds, depressions and other changes in the shape of the ground surface can be exciting, giving interest and individuality to a garden which might otherwise be relatively boring. Let your imagination run free and you might just surprise yourself with your own creativity.

Earth shaping does need to be done the right way, though. Getting the ground levels right is the first job when developing a garden. Consider:

- When you change levels you change drainage patterns, and that could create water build-up or erosion in places where you didn't have such problems earlier.
- When you move earth, you remove the protective cover of plants/weeds and make erosion more likely (until new plants grow); you also remove and relocate topsoil which changes soil fertility and vertical (downwards) drainage.
- Earth used to form mounds or as fill will settle to a lower level (consolidate) over time. Mounds may become smaller than you had in mind, or depressions may occur.

How to do the work

Small earthmoving jobs in easy-to-dig soils can be readily done with a barrow and shovel. Most small jobs, though, will benefit from additional rotary hoeing to loosen the soil (especially clay soils). It will then be easier to work the soil with a shovel.

Medium to large jobs (anything requiring movement of more than a couple of cubic metres of soil) will be easier with the use of some type of earthmoving machinery.

Bobcat

A small machine with rubber tyres and a tractor bucket on the front. The bucket can lift and carry loose soil, rocks, sand etc. It can dig in soil to some extent, but not as much as some other machines. It is more likely to get bogged in wet or loose soil than a backhoe or dozer. Being the smallest (and often the cheapest to hire) a bobcat is most appropriate in confined spaces around a house on a small block (often it is the only machine small enough to gain access to the backyard).

Backhoe

Larger than a bobcat, with a bucket on the front and a digging scoop on a moveable arm at the back. It can do everything that a bobcat can do, and more. It is better at digging, it can dig trenches for pipes or foundations and can place rocks easier and more precisely than a bobcat or dozer. It has rubber tyres like a bobcat and can easily get bogged, particularly in wet soil, but can use its digging arm to pull itself out.

Dozer

This machine moves on 'tracks' (like an army tank) rather than rubber wheels. It is not prone to getting bogged like a backhoe or bobcat and is able to work on steeper slopes than wheeled machines. It has a bucket or blade on the front and is good for digging and shaping the ground, but not always good for moving materials or for trenching.

Experience counts!

When you hire a machine, hire it with a driver who is experienced. A good driver will do three times as much work in the same period of time as an inexperienced worker. Generally half a day should get most of the earthmoving and other heavy work done in an average new home garden. This might involve:

- some cut-and-fill work to terrace a part of the garden;
- establishing the basic levels for the lawn areas;
- bringing soil and mulch from where it was delivered at the front and dumping it in different parts of the garden for use later;
- placing large boulders in position where they might be later used.

Ask a few different contractors for references from past clients, and talk with people who used them before deciding whom to employ. Doing this could save you hundreds of dollars on your earthmoving bill.

Creating mounds

Mounds can add visual interest to most gardens; they are an easy way to utilise excess soil that may be present from other activities such as building site works. Mounds are often used to provide visual barriers or physical barriers to limit access and reduce excess noise. They are also useful in providing variation to children's play areas and also as a means of providing improved drainage for plants that may not be suited to the area's original drainage characteristics. Slight mounds can be grassed over, but generally they are better planted. Ground covers should be used if you want to show the line of the mound, otherwise use shrubs and trees that will appreciate the improved drainage.

When making mounds, a few simple rules should be followed to obtain the best results:

- Never have more than a 30° slope on the mound.
- Mulch the surface of the mound if the slope is over 15°.

- Don't use rocks, asphalt or concrete etc. as fill—they can gradually work to the surface.
- It's best not to use heavy clay as fill, particularly where the overlying soil is lighter in texture.
- If putting lighter soil on top of clay, form the clay underneath to provide the right shape for sub-surface drainage before filling—water must be able to freely drain away.
- Heavy clay on top of heavy clay can be OK.
- If using a mixture of filling material, put the lighter (sandier) soil on top.
- Surface any mound with at least 8 cm of good topsoil.

Fill required for different sized mounds (approximate)
1 m high in centre; 7 m long x 4 m wide requires 15–18 cu. metres
1.7 m high, 6 m wide x 10 m long requires 50–60 cu. metres
2.8 m high, 10 m wide and 18 m long requires 200–230 cu. metres
Note: a 10-ton truck will carry approximately 8 cu. metres.

Where to get filling
- Local council Building or Engineering Departments may help.
- Roadworks
- Swimming pool companies (fill from pool excavations)
- Excavations for dams in rural or semi-rural areas
- Private housing estate developers

Bringing in soil from elsewhere
It is a common practice for landscapers to bring soil into a garden from elsewhere (e.g. for fill, or topsoil for garden beds and lawns). This can lead to some problems:
- You may bring new pests, diseases or weeds into the garden.
- The new soil might not be as good as it looks (e.g. sandy loams are sometimes contaminated with salt, even though they look good).
- If the imported soil has just been placed on the surface of existing soil, without some of the new soil being cultivated into the original soil as a transitional layer, you are likely to have plants sending their roots down through the imported soil and hitting a hard pan underneath, making it difficult for roots to penetrate; or water just passes through the top soil and sits on the surface of the underneath soil, creating waterlogged conditions.

How to build raised beds
Many plants die because they get wet feet due to poor drainage. A raised bed is an easy way to overcome the 'wet feet' problem and at the same time give a relatively flat garden a lot of character.

Rules
- If the raised bed has a wall (e.g. sleepers or stones) retaining the soil, there

should be plenty of drainage holes in the base to allow excess water to drain away.

- If the bed does not have a wall, the edges should be made to minimise any chance of erosion (i.e. they should not be steep, or perhaps rocks, mulch or fast-growing ground covers should be used).
- The soil in the mound should drain well, but should also hold enough moisture to supply plant needs (i.e. ideally a sandy loam mixed with manure, compost or some other organic material).
- Large mounds might benefit from drainage pipes being laid on top of the original soil under the mound to help water move out more quickly from the centre of the mound in wet weather.

Naming the soil

It is useful to know what type of soil you are working with—they are usually named according to texture. Work through the following steps to classify your soil:

1. Place a small quantity of soil in the palm of your hand and add just enough water to make it pliable and easily moulded. Does it:

    1. Stain your fingers   Yes or No?
    2. Bind together   Yes or No?
    3. Feel gritty   Yes or No?
    4. Feel silky or sticky   Yes or No?
    5. Make water cloudy   Yes or No?

2. One or more of the above characteristics will reveal the soil type, as follows:

	1.	2.	3.	4.	5.
a. Sand	NO	NO	YES	NO	NO
b. Sandy loam	NO	YES	YES	NO	NO
c. Loam (or silt)	NO	YES	NO	NO	NO
d. Clay loam	YES	YES	NO	NO	YES
e. Clay	YES	YES	NO	YES	YES

3. You should also be able to distinguish by the amount of grittiness whether it is a coarse, medium, fine or very fine sand. You will also be able to determine varying grades of other soil types by how well they bind together, etc. For example, a clay will bind so tightly that it can be rolled into a ball and formed into shapes (like potter's clay).

Organic soils have a large proportion of organic matter (more than 25%). These are usually black or brown in colour and feel silky. It is possible to get organic types of all of the above soils. Organic soils may be distinguished from others by placing a small amount in a glass of water—if most of it floats on top, then it is an organic soil.

Soil structure

Soil structure refers to the arrangement of mineral particles in soil into larger aggregates known as peds or crumbs. A well structured soil will have good drainage, good aeration, and be easily worked (cultivated). Soil structure usually changes from the surface of the soil as you move deeper down into the earth. One reason for this is that surface soil usually contains more organic matter than deeper soil. Surface layers frequently drain better; drainage rate decreases as you get deeper. This natural change means that water moves quickly away from the surface of soil but slows down its rate of flow as you get deeper. Bad soil cultivation procedures can damage this characteristic gradation in soil structure by destroying the structure at the surface. Heavy foot or vehicle traffic can also cause compaction of surface layers. This may result in increased surface runoff during rainfall and irrigation, and therefore reduced levels of water reaching the roots of plants, as well as poor aeration.

Soil structure can be maintained or improved in the following ways:

1. By cultivating the soil to break up clods, hard pans, etc. Over-cultivation, however, leads to a break-down in structure, as does cultivation when the soil is overly wet.
2. By adding materials such as well rotted organic matter and gypsum.
3. By minimising compaction of the soil by such things as regular foot and vehicle traffic.

DRAINAGE

Over-wet ground is undesirable in any landscape because:

a) it is unhealthy for plant life (promotes pests and disease, reduces oxygen availability to plant roots, increases humidity, etc.).
b) water can go stagnant (and become unhealthy/smelly);
c) ground can become inaccessible (slippery, soggy etc).

To ensure water does not build up in an area you must:

1. prevent water that collects on higher ground from flowing to low spots in the landscape (where it tends to build up);
2. ensure that rainwater moves through the topsoil quickly (i.e. the topsoil has the ability to absorb water and pass it through to deeper layers of the soil);
3. remove water from the sub-soil quickly (by either passing through to even deeper layers or by collecting it in drains so that it flows away from the site).

Drainage can be tested easily by observing the way in which water moves through soil that has been placed in a pot and watered. However, when soil is disturbed by digging, its characteristics may change. Another and more reliable way is to remove the top and bottom from a tin can so that it forms a tube that can be pushed into the soil to a depth of about 8–10 cm. Care should be taken to disturb the soil as little as possible. Water can then be poured into the top of the can and allowed to drain down through the soil. The drainage (or infiltration rate) can then be easily measured in terms of millimetres (mm) of water that soaks into the soil per hour or, more simply, the amount the water level drops, measured in millimetres, in the can each hour.

This can vary considerably according to the type of soil, from zero infiltration in water repellent sands, up to hundreds of millimetres per hour in coarse sands. As the soil becomes wetter the infiltration rate decreases until it reaches a constant rate. For some soils this may take only 15 or 20 minutes, for others it may take many hours. If this constant rate is very low, i.e. a few millimetres per hour, then even light rains will cause surface runoff, and water will accumulate in surface depressions.

Table 7.1 gives an indication of the differences that occur in drainage rates for various soils.

TABLE 7.1. DRAINAGE RATES FOR VARIOUS SOILS	
Soil type	**Constant infiltration rate (millimetres per hour)**
Deep sands, aggregated silts	More than 20
Deep sandy loams	10–20
Clay loams, shallow sandy loams, soils low in organic matter	5–10
Clays	1–5
Sodic clay soils*	Less than 2

(From: *Growing Media for Ornamental Plants and Turf*, Handreck, K and Black, N. NSW University Press, 3rd edn. 1994

*Sodic clay soil is a predominantly clay soil that contains at least 15% sodium, which interferes with plant growth

Improving drainage

Drainage can be improved in a number of ways. These include:
- Increasing the infiltration rate of water into the soil by improving the structure of the soil.
- Provision of sub-surface drainage to facilitate removal of water from the soil, e.g. agricultural pipes.
- Provision of surface drainage to remove surface runoff efficiently.

Improving water infiltration

Infiltration can be improved by:

• Overcoming compaction of the soil.

• Improving soil structure.

• Breaking up impermeable layers in the soil, such as heavy clays.

• Breaking or opening up impermeable surface layers or crusts.

• Overcoming the water-repelling characteristic of some soils (e.g. fine sands).

Methods that can be used to overcome these problems are:

Cultivation. Surface crusting, impermeable layers and compaction can be rectified to some degree by either machine or hand cultivation. For small jobs, hand cultivators (hand forks, trowels, etc.) can be used to overcome surface crusting and spades can be employed to break up the upper soil layers. For large areas, and problems deeper in the soil profile, deep ripping cultivators such as mole ploughs can be very effective.

Rotary hoeing of the topsoil is generally ineffective (particularly on silt soils). This method can make soil more workable in the short term, but may increase drainage problems in the long term by causing a hard, impermeable layer below the level of cultivation.

In cases where sub-soil drainage is installed, it may be necessary to undertake special sub-soil cultivations.

Mixing in soil additives. These are materials that are mixed with the soil to improve its physical structure with respect to its capacity to drain.

Sand. Ideally 70% of soil content should be medium or fine sand particles. This is generally only practical for small areas such as garden beds.

Organic matter. Peat, compost, etc. can help improve soil structure and add valuable nutrients to the soil.

Chemical treatments. These are substances which are applied to improve the soil's chemical characteristics with respect to drainage ability.

Liquid clay breakers. These make clay soils drain more freely. Bought as a concentrated liquid, it is mixed with water and watered onto the ground. It is easier to use than the following treatments.

Lime. This white powder does the same job as clay breaker, but also has side effects—it raises the level of calcium (which can be beneficial but sometimes is a problem) and it makes the soil less acid (raises pH). Unlike clay breaker, lime should be physically dug in to give the best effect.

Gypsum. This does the same as lime but doesn't alter the pH. Gypsum is also useful in soils that have salinity problems as the calcium and magnesium in gypsum replace sodium ions which are attached to soil particles, allowing the sodium to be readily leached out of the soil.

Dolomite lime. This does the same as lime but also adds the nutrient magnesium, which can be an advantage in some situations and a disadvantage in others.

Wetting agents. When applied to soil, these chemicals help improve water infiltration into soils that are water repelling (e.g. some fine sands).

To have an effect, all of these treatments require moist soil conditions over several months, so don't expect instant results.

Provision of sub-surface drains

A sub-surface drain is a pipe buried below the ground surface which collects water and moves it away. Sub-surface drains are rarely needed in sandy soils, but may be very important in heavy clay soils.

Distance between drainage pipes varies, but in heavy clay spacings of 3–5 metres might be necessary, whereas in average soils distances of 6–9 metres are adequate. In wet spots, it may be necessary to add an additional line and decrease the spacing.

Gradients

A drain should never have a slope less than 1:300. In large areas it is advisable that it never be less than 1:200 if possible, or even 1:100 in smaller areas. The slope of a drain should be uniform. Sharp bends should be avoided.

Layout of drains

Herringbone. Lateral drains feed from two sides into a central main drain. This system has the advantage of minimising the depth at which some of the drains need to be placed. If there is likely to be any subsidence after construction, laterals should be kept at less than 30 m in length; on undisturbed ground, up to 90 m lengths could be acceptable.

Grid. Laterals all run into one main drain from one side. This is less complicated than herringbone, has less junctions, and the main drain can run along the boundary, minimising interference with the main parts of the landscape.

Outlets

Any drain must have a low point to which the water can be drained, such as a stormwater drain or creek. If it is impossible to find such an outfall, there are two possibilities:

• Pump the water from the outlet to a suitable disposal point.
• Create a soakaway pit. This is a large, deep hole filled with porous material such as sand or stones; the water collects in this hole and slowly disperses into the surrounding soil.

Depth of drains

There is no firm rule, although a depth of 600 mm is usually considered reasonable. If sub-soil cultivation or sand slitting might be carried out at a future date, it is advisable to place drains deeper (750 mm).

Types of drains

Clay pipes. Rigid; should be covered with stones; are generally long term. Water soaks through the porous pipe and between joins; joins can sometimes allow soil in, causing blockages. Clay pipes have, in recent years, been almost completely superseded by plastic pipes.

Corrugated plastic. Flexible; should be covered with stones. Water soaks through holes in the pipe. The plastic can break down after a number of years.

Fibreglass strip drain. Flexible; stones are optional; water permeates through outer case. A relatively new type of drain, so long-term effects are unknown.

PVC pipe. Rigid; cover with stones; water enters through slits. Generally long term. Slippery surface tends to reduce blocking.

Laying the drain

1. Dig the trench (you must achieve an appropriate, even slope on the base).
2. Lay a thin layer (1–2 cm) of coarse material on the bottom of the trench to keep the pipes clear of the soil and to reduce the likelihood of soil blocking the entry of water into the pipe.
3. Lay and connect the drainage pipes in the bottom of the trench.
4. Cover the pipes with a coarse material. Suitable materials are hard graded clinker or 1–2 cm (half- or three-quarter-inch) screened stone, or 2 cm (three-quarter inch) scoria (free of fine-dust material). This material should fill 30–50% of the trench.
5. Place old newspapers, weed mat, hessian or similar material over the screenings. This helps prevent the movement of fine materials downwards, which would reduce the drainage rates by blocking up gaps between the coarse material.
6. Place a layer of sand over the material protecting the screenings (to fill within a few centimetres of the top of the trench.
7. Cover the sand with a well draining topsoil.

Surface drainage

Provision of surface drainage is also important, particularly where you may have large volumes of surface runoff, possibly from non-porous surfaces such as concrete, paving, asphalt, etc. This can often be simply achieved by sloping surfaces within the landscape so that surface water is directed to a place where it won't cause any harm or it can be efficiently disposed of: perhaps an opening leading into a sub-surface stormwater drain, or to a surface drain.

These drains can in turn connect with larger drains or with natural drainage features such as creeks. Surface drains can be simply constructed by creating an elongated dish-shaped depression or trench in the soil; this can be left naturally grassed or lined with some material such as asphalt or concrete. Pre-formed concrete, clay or plastic open drains are also readily obtainable. These are generally half circle or rectangular in shape. They can be simply slotted together or butted up against each other to provide an even slope of sufficient gradient for the free flow of water.

Improving surface drainage after construction

Sand slitting. Provision of vertical channels through which surface water can flow quickly. This normally involves cutting 1-4 cm wide slits (filled with sand) across the slope at an angle to sub-drains, allowing water to move quickly into these drains. Special machinery such as a ditch witch is used. Sand is fed into the slits through a hopper.

Aerating. A long-term process of spiking and sanding (repeated applications lead to an increase in sand percentage in the soil).

Sub-soiling. Using single deep tine cultivators to rip the sub-soil. This can cause damage to the surface of the ground and repair work becomes necessary.

A checklist for drainage designers

• Are there any council regulations regarding drainage provisions? For example are there specific drainage easements on the property (or adjacent properties) into which surface or subsurface water can be discharged? Do you need permission to connect to existing drainage systems, etc? Check with your local council or drainage board.

• Will the construction of your landscape design interfere with the drainage patterns of adjoining properties? For example, problems can arise from blocking the natural movement of water from higher properties or directing increased volumes of water into adjoining properties.

• Is the drainage system adequate to cope with an unusually heavy or prolonged period of rain?

MULCHES

Mulches are valuable because they:

• reduce the need for watering (by preventing evaporation from the soil surface);
• minimise temperature fluctuation in the root zone, thus helping to keep roots cool in summer and warm in winter;
• help control weed growth;
• reduce wind and water erosion;
• improve the appearance of a garden;
• reduce compaction of the soil by providing a protective barrier;
• add valuable nutrients to the soil if organic mulch materials are used.

How to lay mulch

Before putting down mulch material it is important to get levels and drainage right, and to eradicate weeds (spray with Roundup or Zero and leave for 7–14 days).

General rules
- Most organic materials that haven't been composted will draw nitrogen from the soil. Used as a mulch, they starve plants of nutrients, therefore you need to apply a side dressing of slow-release nitrogen around the base of plants (e.g. with straw, hay, shavings, leaf litter, etc.)
- A layer of newspaper underneath reduces the thickness of mulch needed and thus saves money.
- Mulch should be shallower around the base of plant, creating a basin around the plant stem. If this is not done, mulch can cause collar rot.
- Find out which mulching materials are available in your locality. The type of mulch available, and the cost, varies from place to place.
- Some mulches settle to form a thinner layer (you put it on 20 cm thick and after a month it is likely to be only 10 cm thick).

Table 7.2. Mulches

Type	Cost	Comments
Woodshavings	Cheap	Sawmills, also look under 'Sawdust' in Yellow Pages. Avoid too much fine dust in the shavings; settles to thinner layer. Medium lasting, taking several years to decompose.
Woodchip	Medium	Good in forestry areas and nearby cities. Can vary in quality and appearance from splinters to chunks. Long lasting, semi-permanent having a very slow rate of decomposition.
Straw	Medium	Better in rural areas. Often contaminated with grass seeds. Only lasts one season, decomposing relatively fast.
Lucerne hay	Medium	Better in rural areas. In garden packs in some cities. Unlikely to have weed seeds. Looks good and works well. Usually only lasts one season, or two if laid on thick.
Seaweed	Not sold	Though generally not sold, it can be collected from the seaside. Needs to be washed to remove salt, then it becomes a very good mulch. A good source of micronutrients.
Leaves	Not sold	Collected from below deciduous trees in autumn. Eucalypt and conifer leaves have toxins that harm some plants. Some leaves may last longer than others.

Lawn clippings	Not sold	Easy to collect when mowing Decomposes very fast. This can cause nitrogen deficiency if used in thick layers. Best used only 1 cm thick and topped up every few months as it rots.
Manure	Cheap to medium	Good. Can burn if too thick. A short term mulch. Can bring weed seeds.
Black plastic	Cheap	Very good. Only suitable on raised beds (e.g. as used with strawberries). Can sweat underneath, becoming smelly. If top isn't washed clean by rain it collects dust in which weeds can grow. Stops rain wetting soil below; plants can become too dry under plastic.
Synthetic mulch fabrics	Medium to expensive	Readily available. Long lasting. Their appearance isn't always what is desired. Can be covered with a thin layer of bark for effect.
Paper	Cheap	Readily available. Used either shredded or as sheets. Can be covered with bark for better effect. Rots down in 1–4 years, depending on thickness
Compost	Cheap to expensive	Some types (e.g. spent mushroom compost) can be in good supply and very cheap in some places. Well rotted compost is a good source of nutrients and a very good general mulch. It does not necessarily deter weeds: some composts may be contaminated with weed seeds.
Peat	Expensive	Generally good Very acidic, thus not good on lime-loving plants.
Pine bark	Medium	Good in states with large pine plantations. Can contain toxins if too fresh. Should be well composted before use. Larger, chunky bark lasts longer but doesn't look as good as finer milled material.

Note: The comments above are generalisations. Things do vary from place to place and some details might be quite different in some parts of the country

HARD SURFACING

Hard-surfaced areas are more accessible, remaining dry in winter and dust free in summer, and provide a stable surface for garden furnishings and outdoor living. The materials most commonly used to create hard surfaces are pavers, concrete, and gravel.

Paving

The list of paving materials ranges from various forms of stone (e.g. sandstone slabs, bluestone and cobblestones), to bricks, concrete pavers and timber blocks. Each has a different look about it, and a different price range. You are wise to shop around, look at the alternatives, and perhaps bring a few samples away with you to examine in their potential environment.

Methods for laying pavers

For all types of pavers you need a solid base, otherwise they will rise or subside in line with the movement of the underlying material. This may cause the paved surface to become uneven, perhaps with protruding edges that may make the area unsafe to walk upon. It may also result in depressions that will hold water. Where underlying sediments are very soft or moist you may need to improve drainage by the use of agricultural drains or a layer of rubble or coarse material.

In most situations pavers are laid on a weak mortar base, (i.e. 1 part cement

Cement mixers will be used for rock and paving fixing, structure foundations, water creek creations, etc.

to 4 parts sand) or directly onto a soft sand base that has been firmed down but not packed down too hard. When laying pavers on sand you need to have some sort of border or edge, such as treated timber or a line of bricks set in mortar, that will help hold the sand in position. This edge can be visible or buried just below the surface.

The sand should be tamped down with a hand tamper or, for larger areas, a roller. Straight edges or wooden boards can be used to slide forward and backwards across the sand to get a level surface. The final sand layer should be around 58 cm thick. The pavers should then be pressed securely in position on the sand or mortar base and tapped down level with a straight edge. Consideration should be given to having a slight even slope to the finished surface to aid drainage. The gaps between the pavers can be filled with grout such as the 1 to 4 mortar mix used for bases. The excess grout should be wiped clean or brushed away with a stiff-bristled broom.

When the paved area is to be used for vehicle access or other heavy uses, then the pavers should be laid on a more substantial base, such as an 8 cm layer of reinforced concrete.

Equipment for paving
If you plan to do your own paving you will need the following:
A *spirit level* is essential when paving to allow for water runoff. Provide a small gradient away from the centre of the paving and install a collection and drainage system.
A *string line* ensures that the pavers are laid in straight lines.
A *soft headed hammer* or rubber mallet is used for positioning pavers and making them snug and tight. Should one paver rise a little too high it can easily be hammered down.
A *vibrating plate* (optional) is used to hammer pavers into place once they have been laid. Hiring this machine makes large paving jobs easier and saves time.

Concrete

Despite the distaste many people have for concrete, it remains probably the most popular surfacing material. It is relatively inexpensive, long lasting and, if laid properly, perhaps the easiest surface to maintain. Concrete can be finished in the following ways to create different effects:
- by adding pigment to change the colour;
- by brushing the surface lightly with a stiff broom to create a non-slip surface;
- by use of moulds to create cobblestone or effects.

Laying a concrete path
1. Dig out the area to be concreted, usually 12–14 cm deep.
2. Compact the base of this dug area with a roller or ramming machine.

3. Add a layer of gravel, stones or sand (6–8 cm deep), rake over to obtain required levels and compact with a roller or ramming machine.

4. Peg wooden planks along the sides of the path, with the top of the planks set at the final level you intend for the path. Allow for concrete to be at least 6 cm thick, and much thicker if vehicles are to be driven over it.

5. Pour concrete a small section at a time. Use a long, smooth board rested on the side planks for levelling. Using a sawing motion, gradually work this board along the side planks, moving the concrete to achieve the required level, and create as smooth a surface as possible.

6. Sprinkle a mixture of sand and cement (4 to 1) over the surface of the path and, using concrete trowels, smooth the surface to remove any holes or blemishes.

7. Using a metal bar, make an expansion joint at least every 1.5–2 metres along the path. This is an indentation in the surface to prevent cracking due to expansion and contraction in extreme weather conditions).

Concrete mix for paths and driveways should comprise 2 parts cement:3 parts sand:5 parts stones (approximately 1 cm [half inch] aggregate).

Concreting know-how

- Concrete is stronger if it dries slowly. Covering it with damp hessian or wet newspaper will slow down the drying rate.
- Setting-retardant chemicals can be added to slow down the rate of drying.
- It is not advisable to lay concrete in very hot, rainy or frosty weather.
- In rain, freshly laid concrete should be carefully covered with plastic sheeting.
- Concrete reaches full strength slowly:

After 2 hours: Workable; no strength at all.
After 3 days: No longer workable, still has very little strength, easy to damage.
After 7 days: Solid, still only half strength.
After 30 days: Very solid, full strength.

Gravelled areas

If cash is limited, gravel is generally the choice. Gravel is crushed rock (preferably screened or sieved). Gravelled areas can look very good if constructed properly, and if you use a good quality gravel. The best gravel is one that has an even texture (i.e. no large rocks or lumps) and contains enough fine material to make it 'set'. A gravel that doesn't contain 'fines' will always remain loose and will become a nuisance (i.e. gravel will spread inside the house, onto lawns, paved areas and everywhere else). A well constructed gravel area should have a slope over its surface so that water will drain off the area to one or both sides, but not along its length (which will cause erosion).

RETAINING WALLS

As the name implies the aim of a retaining wall is hold back earth. Common uses for retaining walls are:

- to stabilise an embankment or slope, particularly after excavation for building or road construction;
- to stabilise sandy areas such as dunes;
- to create raised garden beds;
- to create embankments for terracing;
- to provide bank protection against erosion for water features such as small streams and large ponds.

Retaining walls have to contend with pressure from soil behind the wall, particularly during wet weather. The wall must slope backwards from the base (i.e. have a 'batter') if it is to cope with this pressure, and there should be adequate drainage to allow water behind the wall to escape. High walls should have inbuilt drainage holes, and sometimes even drainage pipes laid in stones behind the wall.

Design considerations

The designer should consider the following:

Shape and substance of the wall

Ideally, the wall should follow as closely as possible the shape of the embankment it is retaining, to avoid carting large quantities of soil either into or out of the work site. The substance from which the wall is built is largely determined by what materials are available.

- Dry walls (without cementing) need a solid base/foundation.
- A mortared wall needs a concrete strip foundation and weep-holes for drainage.

The 'batter'

All walls should slope back into the embankment (i.e. 'the batter'). A minimum batter should be approximately 1 cm for every 10 cm in height.

Ideally, the ground at both the top and bottom of a wall should be fairly flat, to minimise erosion.

Drainage above and below

Obviously, this factor is more critical in clay soils. A spoon drain may be built at both the top and bottom of the wall. Sub-surface drains might also be used in these positions.

If surface drainage is allowed to run over the top of the wall, it can very quickly cause bad erosion behind and at the base of the wall.

Materials for retaining walls

Timber, brick, cut stone (e.g. bluestone), bush rock and concrete are among the materials that are commonly used in the construction of retaining walls.

Timber walls

Timber is generally suited to retaining walls that are no more than about 1–1.2 metres in height. A low retaining wall or edge piece can be created simply by drilling holes through a sleeper and banging pieces of water pipe, steel rod or similar material through the sleeper and into the ground beneath to anchor it.

For higher walls, timber uprights spaced about 2 metres apart are anchored in the ground to retain a wall of horizontally placed timber pieces. In some cases the uprights are placed so that the ends of two adjoining sleepers will butt up against each other behind the upright so that the joins are not visible.

Upright timbers need to be secured into the ground, usually with concrete and preferably leaning at a slight angle towards the hill. If set only in soil, the uprights should be set about the same depth into the ground as the height of the wall above ground; if set in concrete, they should be set about 50–60 cm deep. Vertical timbers can be secured into place by using hot dipped galvanised bolts or sleeper nails.

Hardwood

This is a versatile material. Some Australian hardwood timbers such as red gum, grey gum, yellow gum and grey ironbark are quite durable. Freshly milled

Sleeper wall.

timber of this type is available in a variety of sizes. Second-hand, weathered timber of this type is sometimes available, particularly when old buildings are demolished.

The most common type of hardwood timber used is red gum in the form of railway sleepers. These can be purchased as second-hand (having the advantage of a well-weathered, natural appearance) or freshly milled, generally having a more regular form (i.e. straight edges, smoother finish) making them easier to lay. Sleepers are generally available in lengths ranging from 2.3 m (8 ft) to 3.0 m (10 ft) and are usually about 23 cm (9 inches) wide by about 13 cm (5 inches high). Half standard thickness 'sleepers' have been specially milled for landscaping purposes. These have the same length and width of a standard sleeper but only about half the weight.

Softwood
Treated pine is often used for low retaining walls. It is cheap, versatile and easy to work with, being lighter than hardwood. Pine won't take as much knocking as hardwood, though, and will rot quickly unless preservative is properly applied. Treated pine can last quite a while and is available through companies such as Koppers as pre-made interlocking 'crib' type walling.

Equipment and tools for timber wall construction
To make the holes for the bolts, a *drill* is required. Ensure that your drill machine and bit are strong enough for the job. Cordless drills are not strong enough for such a large job.

Electric saw. Hardwood and softwood timber are both easily cut with electric saws. Once again, the power of the machine and the size of the blade must be appropriate for the job at hand. Should you be using round logs, then a chain saw will be needed as well as a good grasping bench or implement to securely hold the log as you cut. Be very careful, as these tools can be dangerous. Old sleepers can damage chain saws, therefore it is wise to have a spare cutting chain at hand in case one breaks or if the job is likely to take more than one hour of cutting.

Masonry or rock walls
The two main methods of building masonry or rock walls are:

Dry walls. These are built by stacking rocks or blocks one on top of another without using concrete or any other 'joining' material to stick them together. The individual units need to be stacked in such a way that they interlock as much as possible; with a decent batter, a good deal of stability is achieved. The base of this type of wall should be twice as wide as the main section of the wall. This spreads the weight and helps prevent the wall sinking.

Wet walls. Stones or blocks are concreted together to form wet walls. A strip foundation should be laid first, with steel reinforcing set in concrete; the stones/ blocks are then laid on top.

To further strengthen the wall, sections of wall are run back into the embankment at intervals. These walls can be effectively cemented with a mortar mix of 3 parts fine sand to 1 part cement.

Brick walls

New or old bricks can be used for brick walling. Though not as natural in appearance as timber, stones or rocks, bricks come in a wide variety of colours and textures suited to most styles of garden, and a brick wall is quite strong if well laid.

To build a brick wall you will need a trowel, a string line, a bricklayer's hammer (with a chisel end), a spirit level and a shovel (to mix cement).

Pre-cast concrete wall blocks

Specially shaped interlocking blocks for forming retaining walls are now widely available through larger masonry companies. These are available in a variety of shapes and colours and are particularly easy to lay in position, but are heavy to lift. They produce a very durable wall and many are designed to allow for planting holes. A solid base is required, and care must be taken to ensure that the bottom layer is level. Once this is done it is easy to simply lay the rest of the layers on and keep them level.

Dry stone wall under construction.

ROCKERIES

In European and American gardens, rockeries aim to reproduce the effect seen in alpine areas, where low-growing plants are found amongst rocky outcrops.

Rockeries in Australian bush gardens might follow a similar style, attempting to recreate the effects found in the high country of Tasmania or south-eastern Australia, with clumping plants and small shrubs (including grasses, daisies etc.) growing amongst rocky outcrops.

Rocks have been used in native bush gardens in many ways, including:

- rocky outcrops created as erosion control in sloping areas;
- outcrops or clusters of rocks at focal points, used as an interesting visual feature;
- rocks around pools or ponds;
- flat rocks used to provide a seemingly natural all-weather walkway (e.g. in a watercourse or within a garden bed, allowing access to places which would otherwise be inaccessible without damaging plants).
- large rocks used to shelter unstable plants—when planted alongside large rocks, the plants gain stability as the roots grow under the rock and take advantage of the fact that these spots do not dry out as fast as more exposed soil.

Rockeries require a fair bit of pre-planning and construction. You need to ensure an adequate supply of rock material and soil fill, and that they are well weathered rocks that will give a natural appearance in the rockery. Ideally, the rocks should

Rocks are generally moved by bobcats or front end loaders such as this.

be buried at least half to two-thirds into the soil, with only weathered surfaces exposed. Arrange the first foundation layer of rocks as desired and fill in the area with soil, then progressively work through the rocks and soil as you add them to the garden. In arranging the rocks, remember to leave open areas for plant growth. Once the construction phase has been completed, water well and allow the area to settle naturally before planting.

Equipment used

Moving rocks and soil is made much easier with the use of a *Bobcat* (optional). If you are only using small rocks, a good quality wheelbarrow can be used instead. *Crowbar* to wriggle or position the rock where it is most suitable in the rock garden.

Shovel for moving soil into position around the rocks.

Artificial rocks

It is possible to simulate the effect of rocks in a garden, using concrete constructions. This type of work has the following advantages over working with real rocks:

- You do not have the tough work of moving heavy boulders about (though mixing concrete can be hard work).
- You are not damaging natural environments by removing rocks that may be an integral part of natural ecosystems.
- You are not restricted to using only rocks of a size that can be moved.
- You can create any shape and size you wish to create.
- Crevices for planting, water courses, pools etc, can be created where and in the form that is desired.

If created properly, artificial rocks will look just as natural as the real thing. Components used in the surface layer will create a texture and colour that simulates natural formations. The procedure is as follows:

Shaping. Create a mound of sand or soil in the shape of the boulder or rock cluster that you plan to build. This is often done by filling plastic or hessian bags with sand or soil and stacking in the desired shape.

Reinforcing layer. A layer of wire mesh (e.g. chicken wire) is spread over the surface of the shaped form.

Base cement layer. A layer of cement or concrete 6–10 cm thick is spread over the chicken wire. Ensure that this mix is not too moist, so that it will hold firm where it is applied. If the concrete begins to slump in near vertical sections, it may be necessary to lean bags of sand or soil against those sections as support until they dry.

If this procedure is carried out in hot weather, it will be necessary to keep the concrete moist by either hosing or covering it with wet hessian, in order to slow down drying. It needs to dry slowly in order to be strong and not crack. Similarly, if heavy rain is expected the work should be covered with plastic for protection.

The cement is applied at this stage using a trowel (or cement worker's float) to spread the cement from the bottom of the structure upwards. When doing steep sections it may be necessary to do a small part at a time, allowing it to dry before returning to the section above. *The surface should not be smooth.* Leave a rough trowelled surface at this first layer. This layer should be strong, giving the necessary structural support required for the final rock.

Final layer. The moment of truth comes when the final layer is rendered (spread over the earlier layer). First place over the initial layer a fine wire mesh (e.g. 12 mm mesh). Use one of the mixes below to spread a 2–3 cm layer over the surface. A day after applying the coat (before it has completely hardened but is firm enough to withstand some knocks), scrub the surface with a steel brush to give it a rough texture. After 3 or 4 days, pick over the surface with a sharp instrument such as a chisel or screw driver to create further textured effects.

Coating mixes

A. To create a simulated coarse surface texture similar to granite:

    8 parts coarse river sand   4 parts fine sand
    2 parts cement   2 parts lime
    1 part mountain soil (preferably a red clay loam)

B. For a smooth sandstone-like effect:

    8 parts fine sand   4 parts coarse river sand
    2 parts cement   2 parts lime
    1 part red or brown clay loam or sandy loam

C. For a more pitted effect:

    8 parts sand (coarse or fine or mixed)   3 parts cement
    2 parts soil   3 parts cement
    2 parts polystyrene balls (i.e. bean bag balls)

A week after setting, wash over the surface with brick cleaning acid. This will dissolve the polystyrene, leaving cavities.

Other additives can be used for different effects:

- Different coloured soils to modify the coloration of the rock.
- Peat moss to also change the colour.

Protect plants

If you are going to plant close to the work, be aware that the concrete is alkaline (i.e. it has a high pH) and will affect the pH of the soil around it as chemical components leach out of the cement. In sandy soil, the effect may wash away through the soil after 6 months or so, but it is wise to test the pH and perhaps compensate for this problem by washing the surface of the rock a few times with a 50/50 solution of vinegar and water.

Water in the Garden

Water can be a most restful and relaxing feature in any garden. In fact, many garden designers around the world consider that a garden without a water feature like a stream, pond, fountain or waterfall is simply not complete.

The biggest problem with water in the garden, however, is in keeping it clean and crystal clear—a stagnant green puddle is good for nothing but the swarms of mosquitos that will quickly invade the area.

Choosing a water garden

The type of water feature you choose to incorporate into your landscape design will depend on a variety of things. You need to consider:

Location

Where you put water depends on its purpose. Usually informal ponds are best located in depressions or low points, never on top of a mound. Formal ponds can be located at high or low points. Streams obviously start at higher ground and run to a lower point. The start and finish of a stream should normally be hidden from view, usually with heavy plantings.

Water features create a focal point in a garden and will be better appreciated where they can be seen from inside the house, or perhaps from an outdoor living area.

Reflections of light are better from water in a sunny spot, though a poorly maintained pond will tend to grow more weed and algae in a sunnier position. Water features can also be attractive in shady areas, such as a fernery, but you are unlikely to get many aquatic plants to flower in shaded conditions.

Cost

Water features do not have to be expensive; cheap prefabricated ponds can be purchased from water garden specialists. On the other hand, it is possible to spend thousands of dollars on large, elaborate water gardens that can transform a garden into a showcase.

Size

The depth of water is important, particularly with ponds. If a pond is too shallow, it is too hard to develop a balanced ecology that will keep the water, animal and plant life in a healthy, self-sustaining condition. Ponds should be at least 35 cm (or 14 inches) deep. This depth is necessary over as much of the pool as possible— just one deep pocket is insufficient. Water lilies and many other aquatic plants will not grow in very shallow water. Fish need deep areas to provide protection against predators such as birds or cats. Shallow ponds are more difficult to keep clean.

The overall dimensions of a water feature are also important; they should 'fit' the scale of the garden. For example, a large pond or fountain will likely look out of place in a small courtyard garden, while it may be extremely difficult to create a balanced ecosystem in a very small pond. The smaller the pool the harder it is to establish fish. As a general rule a fish pond should have minimum surface dimensions of 1.2 x 1 metre.

It should also be remembered that once a pool is installed in the ground it will look about one-third smaller than it did out of the ground, so it is best to carefully measure the size of pool that you want.

Setting up

Plastic or rubber liners are the easiest to install. They are very flexible and can be readily formed to the desired shape. Prefabricated ponds, waterfalls and stream systems made from fibreglass are also fairly easy to install. Concrete requires considerably more construction effort.

Moving or still water?

Moving water can be provided as either a fountain, a waterfall or a flowing stream. Moving water requires a pump and that is an added expense; however, moving water is much easier to keep clean. It is also easier to grow fish and plants in it.

Plants and animals to use

Your choice of water plants and animals will depend on the size, depth and position of the pool. Fish are useful to control mosquitos. Water snails can also be an important part of the ecology of a balanced system. They eat some algae and decaying plant material, but they can be a problem if there are no fish to keep them in check.

Keeping the water in

Water can be held in the following ways:

Concrete

Concrete is often used to line a depression formed in the earth. Waterproofing compounds purchased from a hardware store should be added to the concrete to stop it leaking. After a week of drying, a concrete pond should be filled and left for a month to allow lime in the cement to be removed. That water should then be replaced before planting with water plants and stocking with fish. The concrete should be at least 8 cm or more in thickness. Some sort of reinforcement in the concrete, such as chicken wire mesh, can be beneficial in helping to prevent cracks in the concrete.

Brick or stone

Brick or stone are more commonly used to build formal pools. The pond should be treated as for concrete pools to remove any traces of lime in the water. Unless well constructed, water features made of these materials tend to have leakage problems.

Fibreglass

Prefabricated fibreglass or solid plastic ponds come in all shapes and sizes, but they can be fairly expensive. They can be linked together to create a series of ponds, one flowing into the next, or to create waterfalls, and generally provide the easiest way to add water to a garden. They should be well anchored to prevent them from moving.

Pool liners

These are fabrics (e.g. heavy duty plastics or butynol rubber) that can be laid in the bottom of a hole to hold water. They have the advantage of being easily laid and fairly cheap. They are more likely to be damaged than the other types of liners, but they are fairly readily patched.

Waterproofing the ground

In larger gardens it is possible to create small lakes or dams in holes dug straight into the ground. To help seal the soil and prevent water loss into the subsoil, puddling with lime and clay is the usual waterproofing technique. Without any treatment, water that fills these holes will settle near to the level of the water table. In some places this may be only just below ground level, but very often it is much deeper.

Clean water

Water can be cleaned in three different ways:
1. Using chemicals
2. Using filters
3. Improving the biology of the pond or stream.

Chemical additives may provide a useful solution to a short-term problem, but should not be relied on for long-term control of water quality. Many water purifying chemicals will harm fish, particularly if used repeatedly.

Filters are not always necessary, however in many situations a filter is an easy and effective way to minimise build-up of waste products from fish or the presence of algae.

Filters

Where persistent water quality problems exist—or may be expected—filtration may be the only solution.

Simply circulating the water will achieve little. A fountain or cascade may help add oxygen to water, but this alone will not keep the water clear.

There are two types of filters:

Physical filters. Water is pumped through a physical barrier such as a fine mesh (strainer-like) or fine material such as diatomaceous earth. These filters need to be cleaned regularly. Where sediment levels are very high this type of filter may not be adequate.

Biological filters. Water passes through a bed containing materials such as gravel, scoria and sand in which micro-organisms work on impurities (e.g. algae, dead insect tissue, fish excreta, as well as ammonia and other products of decomposing materials), breaking these elements down and removing them from the water.

Where water clarity is an ongoing problem, the best solution is to install a biological filter.

The key to successful biological filtration, however, lies in proper design. How big should the filter be? What size pump should be used? While there are some basic guidelines that can help, this is a problem that will often require some expert help. First, the filter should be set up separate from the pond and the sand or gravel, etc. should be at least 30 cm deep. The area of the filter should be about one sixth the area of the pond, and the pump should be big enough to handle half the volume of the pond every hour.

It is important to ensure that the water flows evenly through all of the filter material. The best way to do this is to have about 10 cm of free space under the medium to take the incoming water, with the medium sitting on some sort of mesh or screening material. The water will pass up through the medium; the flow of water through the filter should be continuous. The container holding the filter should allow for about 10 cm (in depth) of water to sit above the filtration medium. The water will pass from this area back into the pool, etc. Ideally it should be allowed to fall into the pool over a waterfall, as this will help re-oxygenate the water. The filter should be cleaned about every two years.

To be more precise than this, however, requires a knowledge of how many fish (and even the type of fish) to be kept in the pond, together with the number of plants (if any) that will be allowed to grow.

Hints for landscaping around a pond

- Never use plants with damaging roots.
- Create a more natural effect by covering the edges of a pond where possible with overhanging plants or rocks.
- Be careful to use plants that won't drop a lot of leaves or twigs into the water.
- Provide some open space around a pond so birds can move in and out freely without being ambushed by cats.
- Locate plants or other features (e.g. statues) in a position where you will be able to see their reflection on the water surface.

STEPS

The riser and the tread (horizontal section) of a step always need to bear a comfortable relationship to each other. For instance, if the tread is very narrow and the riser very high, the step becomes difficult and even dangerous to use.

Construction

- Always use a non-slip material. Remember that, while wood and stone might be non-slip, if the steps are not used a lot moss or algae can grow on the surface if they become very wet, and this can be very slippery.
- If the step is in a place which might frequently be wet, and there is a chance it might become slippery at times, install a hand rail.
- Pay attention to drainage. The faster steps drain, the quicker they become dry. A slight slope to the side is important to remove water from the steps (do not slope to the front, as this just redirects water to the next step down).

Materials
Wood can be used, but generally only for the riser. If wood is used for a tread, be cautious of it becoming slippery. Frost on a wooden step can be particularly dangerous.

If wood is used for a riser, concrete, asphalt or gravel might be used for the tread. This may be inexpensive and adequate in a home garden, but not in a public garden.

Concrete is easy to work with and excellent for steps. Do not have a perfectly smooth tread though; it is good practice to put some type of indentation into the surface of each step to give a better grip.

Bricks or pavers. These can be excellent but, once again, pay attention to the grip. If set into concrete, there should be no maintenance problem, but without concrete or cement, there can be two problems:

- The pavers or bricks can move due to disturbance by plant roots or soil subsidence.
- Weeds are likely to grow in cracks between bricks or pavers.

Asphalt is an ideal material for the tread. It is normally used in conjunction with stone, brick or timber risers.

Cut stone such as slate can be used to great effect for steps. You need to check that the stone is not too smooth, otherwise it is likely to be slippery.

8
Managing Finances and Costing

There are plenty of people who are good gardeners or landscapers, and always have lots of work, but still never seem to make much money. There are others who run seemingly smaller businesses, doing less work, but who make much more profit.

'The important thing is not the size of your contract, but the amount that you keep at the end of the job!'

BUSINESS PLANNING

One of the sayings you'll hear often in the commercial world is that businesses don't plan to fail, they fail to plan. While many people appear to just 'fall into' a good business venture and have success without trying, upon closer inspection it is usually their ability to plan and their awareness of the economics of business that make them successful.

Business skills are not something we are born with. This is why planning is essential. For instance, if you intend to start a small part-time business, what is the goal of having that business? Do you hope to build up until you can work full-time and give up other employment? Are you hoping to earn a little extra to purchase something special? Will the money earned go back into the business or go straight into household money? All of these things must be considered and will determine how your business is run. If you are just hoping to make a little extra cash, then you won't want to be reinvesting your earnings into business purchases. If your long-term goal is to be running your own business full-time, then sacrificing things such as a personal salary may be necessary in the early days.

Cash flow, earning projections and other financial data will also be required if you need to approach a lending institution for funds. You not only need to complete these projections to apply for the loan, you also need to make sure they are accurate, so that repayments do not create a hardship for you. Marketing plans are also essential. Many people have wonderful ideas for new business ventures, but cannot make them work if they don't get their business information to the right people. Often, it takes more than a few advertisements in the local newspaper to get business going. You can hope for word-of-mouth business once you are up and going, but the hardest part is getting those first few customers through the door.

Aside from planning on expenditure and earnings, you also need to plan on how the business will affect your lifestyle. The first few years of a business are often critical to the long-term success of the business. They usually require a great deal of commitment beyond the eight hours a day, five days a week we work as employees of another company. Are you ready to make this commitment? More importantly, will your family be ready to support you? They will be sacrificing your contributions to household help and, often, family functions. Without their support, the results can be devastating, regardless of your level of financial planning.

These are just a few of the many things that you, as a prospective business owner, must look at. However, spending a few days on planning can save you a great deal of money and heartache, and can make the difference between failure and success.

COSTING JOBS

Every job begins with a quote. The gardener or landscaper must look at the site, discuss what is needed with the owner, and then propose what work he might do, and what price he might charge. At this point, there are lots of variables (e.g. when the job will be done, and to what standard). Every one of these variables must be considered and made 100% clear before any work commences. Unless this is done, there are likely to be costly disputes later on.

It is also important to get to know your client. There are different types of clients: some are easy to work for, and others can be difficult; and a difficult client can cost you dearly in time, labour and materials.

• Some clients are simply looking for an inexpensive job.
• Some are pedantic or fussy, wanting to repeatedly discuss every fine detail of the job with you.
• Some have very definite ideas of what they want and will not change their idea, even if it is an impractical one.
• Some are very poor communicators.
• Some change their minds about what they want as the work proceeds.
• Some are domineering or condescending, perhaps showing little regard for your knowledge and experience.
• Some are genuinely seeking advice.

Remember: It may be better to miss getting a job, than taking on a project with a difficult client who ends up costing you valuable time and money, as well as creating a lot of stress.

Common mistakes with costing

- Giving a quote based on a gut feeling rather than real figures.
- Not writing down all costs systematically.
- Basing the quote on an over-optimistic scenario.
- Not covering obscure costs such as advertising, taxes, superannuation, loss of work due to wet weather, etc.
- Basing the quote on wages only, and not including profit in the quote.
- Not allowing for increased costs of materials, storm damage, etc.
- Giving a quote only verbally and having nothing to refer to if there is a dispute
- Leaving ambiguities in the contract so it is uncertain who is to pay for some things (e.g. does the client or the contractor pay for removal of rubbish, and for after care of plants?).
- Skill problems (e.g. quoting on a large costly project before developing appropriate knowledge to implement and carry through the project).
- Liquidity problems.
- Depending too heavily on one client (or type of client).
- Failure to allow for contingencies.

How to determine costs and charges for your work

There are several things to be considered when you set a level of fees that you will charge for work:

Materials

This includes such things as chemical sprays, fertiliser, lawn seed, ties and stakes, soil conditioners, landscaping material (e.g. rocks, sleepers, fencing materials, pavers etc), soil, plants, etc. Be sure of your costs. Just because sleepers cost you so much the last time you bought some, only a couple of weeks ago, don't assume they will cost the same when you go to buy them for the current job you are quoting for. Ring around your suppliers and check current prices, and ask also if there are likely to be any price increases forthcoming. Do not forget minor costs. Anything you provide should be charged for.

Equipment costs

Small and large tools and equipment such as rakes, secateurs, wheelbarrows, lawn mowers, chain saws and tractors come under this heading. Use of your vehicle to and from the job and for any errands or deliveries should also be accounted for. Include car, truck, trailer, any road equipment you need for the particular job. Costs can be calculated on an hourly charge rate or a per kilometre rate. It is usually easier to run on-the-job equipment at an hourly rate, while it may be easier to calculate road equipment on a per kilometre basis.

For those items you will be using on the job, you may use as a guide the rates on similar equipment charged by an equipment hire business. However, even if you do use a similar rate, it is best to calculate your own real cost, to ensure you are being reimbursed for the full cost to you. A hire rate can be based upon your estimate of the lifespan of the tool or equipment. For example, you may have a piece of equipment, say a lawn mower, that you expect to last in use for one year. The lifespan for that piece of equipment is 2000 hours if it is in use 40 hours a week for a year, or 1000 hours if it is in use half of the time, etc. Divide the cost of replacing the machine by the lifespan hours. So, if a replacement mower will cost you $700.00, and you intend to use the machine for 2000 hours, the hourly rate for the machine alone is 35 cents. In addition to this, you must include a charge for fuel and maintenance. So, you must determine approximately how much fuel you need to run the machine for the hour, plus maintenance costs for the year. In this exercise, we will allow $500 for maintenance for the year, divided by the 2000 working hours, which is 25 cents. Finally, if the machine needs 1 litre of fuel per hour, at 80 cents per litre, then the total hourly cost to hire or use the lawn mower is $1.40.

Road vehicle travel can be calculated in the same manner, or you can use a per kilometre rate. The tax department has a scheduled rate for cars, based on their engine capacity, and this can be used as a guide. Don't forget to include the cost of running a trailer and the effect this may have on your actual fuel and mileage costs. This will give you the charge-out rate.

Insurance costs

Insurance adds a high cost to running a business. At the very least, all businesses should carry public liability, to ensure that any accidents that occur on the job do not spell the end of the business. If you are employing staff, there will be Workers Compensation insurance, but this will be considered as part of the wage. Other types of insurance including Vehicle (which can be included on your car on-road costs), Contents insurance for the business premises (including rates if you own the property), loss of work for yourself, etc.

Wages

This is the part of your fee that is going to be paid to the person who does the work, whether that person is you or someone whom you employ. This can range from $10 per hour for someone new and inexperienced in the industry, to $30 for someone qualified, experienced and with a good reputation. Wages costs should include all costs of having the employee on the job. This will include Workers Compensation Insurance, Superannuation contributions and tax to be paid. Provision should also be made for leave and sickness entitlements, cost of training, and any necessary safety equipment and work clothing you provide. If you are employing someone, you need to register and pay for them. Or, you may choose to employ staff as sub-contractors. Sub-contractors will normally command a higher rate, as superannuation and tax charges will be paid by them directly. A minimum of 25% over the wage rate should be expected for sub-contractor rates. If you work alone, you need to put aside 25% of your wages towards tax, which is normally paid in a lump sum during the year.

Administration overheads

There are numerous other costs that a business will incur and which should be passed on to the customer. These include:

- The cost of preparing a bill, posting it out, waiting for payment and processing payment when it comes. This includes stationery, postage, labour and possibly collection costs.
- The cost of advertising. This is usually no more than 5% of your annual turnover, although you may find the cost higher in the first year, until your reputation and clientele are more established.
- The cost of printing stationery, business cards, etc. for everyday use.
- The time spent preparing quotations. You may choose to give free quotes, or you may elect to charge for a quote and deduct that fee from the cost of the final job. Regardless of how you approach the quote, the cost of it should be factored in as an administrative overhead.
- The cost of running an office. This includes items such as telephone, utilities, office rent, office furnishings. You should charge for the use of space or office, even if it is a home office. Many people believe that if they own the buildings then they can charge less to the customer. However, if you were not using the space for your own business, you would be using it for something else that would most likely earn income, such as renting out the space, or having a smaller mortgage because, without the need for the office and storage space, you could be comfortable in a smaller home. Having a business space, even if you own it, is a cost to you and must be included in your costings.

Profit

This is what is left after all other things have been paid for. You should try to make a minimum of 10% over your costs on each job. Keep in mind that you have to remain competitive, but working without profit is work not worth doing. You may find early in the business that you are not making the profit you would like, for instance costs may be greater than you first anticipated. However, strive to keep that profit margin on all costings, so that money is on hand to cover extra costs and to put back into the business to allow it to grow.

Note: If you are not making a profit, just making enough to cover your wages and other costs, then you might be better off working for someone else (less risk to you), and investing elsewhere any money you would otherwise have invested in your own business. This way you will at least make some additional profit from your investment.

The first year is always the hardest, as you want to cost your jobs at a competitive rate while still achieving a profit to reinvest and allow the business to grow. Here is where good record keeping will be of great help. By keeping track of all costs, from every stamp purchased to every litre of fuel or maintenance bill, you can, in the second year of business, accurately calculate your costs. This may show you that you need to increase charges, or it may indicate that your profit margin is greater than you had expected. While using last year's results to calculate current costs is ideal, do keep an eye on inflation rates, so that you do not lose out. Costing rates should be reviewed at least once every six months so that changes in things such as fuel and insurance costs can be catered for.

Example

The following example is meant to be only a rough guide to how you can go about calculating a quote for a job. *Please remember that it is an example only—do not use these costings as accurate for the current market.*

The contractor in this instance is someone starting a new lawnmowing business. The job being quoted on is a contract to mow lawns surrounding a shopping centre, with service to be provided weekly.

The contractor estimates that the mowing will require 4 hours' work weekly and the Centre will be billed monthly, payment due 7 days from billing date.

		Hourly Rate
Materials	No materials needed for this job	0.00
Equipment.	Mower (life of 1 yr at 40 hrs per week) replacement cost $700, life 2000 hrs plus fuel and maintenance cost	1.40
Insurance	Hourly rate for all insurances	2.50
Wages	$10 per hr plus $.06 per hour superannuation and $2.50 per hour Workers Compensation plus $1.45 to cover leave and sickness benefits	14.00
Administration	Overheads, rent, billing, etc.	1.00
Profit Margin	10%	1.75
Hourly rate		$20.65

4.333 weeks per month x 4 hrs per week = 17.33 x $20.65/hr = $357.86
(There are 52 weeks in a year, so 4.333 weeks in a month. If you calculate at 4 weeks per month, you will be paid for 48 weeks annually, not 52.)

Billing

It is not uncommon to have to send a second bill, or to be paid late. This costs your business money and the cost should be passed on to the customer. The first bill should be included in your Overheads charge. If you have to send a second bill, and are waiting on payment past the due date, then make an extra charge of approximately $5.50, being $1.00 (hourly rate for administration of sending a new bill) plus $4.50 (approximately) in interest, based on a month's bank interest of 15% on $357.86.

LANDSCAPE SPECIFICATIONS AND CONTRACTS

A landscape specification and contract document can be simple or complex, but whichever it is, it should fulfil three main purposes:

1. As a tender document
It provides a basis upon which a contractor can submit a price for which they are prepared to do the work.

2. As a legal document
It defines the responsibilities of all parties involved in a contract. It must be an exact document, free of ambiguities. If there are any disputes between a client and a contractor, the specifications provide a clear reference for settling the dispute quickly.

3. As a work document
It provides a clear guide as to what should be done on a job.

Example layout of a landscape specification

The following is only a guide, but will provide a framework for preparing a basic specification which, together with a landscape plan, will form the basis upon which to undertake a landscape contract.

You can lay out, include or exclude information as you wish, in any specification. The most important things are to cover all important details (which might lead to disputes if not understood properly from the start), and to present information clearly and free from ambiguity.

1.01 Definitions
e.g. Where the word 'allow' appears the cost of the item is the responsibility of the client (e.g. allow $50).
Excavate shall mean cut and fill.

1.02 Documents
e.g. The accompanying plans drawn by J. Mason on 12/9/89 shall be considered part of this specification.

1.03 Program, Guarantee, Maintenance
e.g. The work will be commenced prior to .... and completed before ....
The contractor shall bear no responsibility for the landscape after completion of work as specified in these documents.
Maintenance of the landscape after completion is the responsibility of the client.

2. TENDERS

2.01 Before tendering the tenderer should visit and examine the site. Claims arising from ignoring this will be invalid.

2.02 Tenders close on ......

2.03 The lowest price will not necessarily be accepted.

3. GENERAL

3.01 The contractor will provide materials, labour and plants necessary for satisfactory completion of works in accordance with the specifications.

3.02 Contingencies: The sum of money $....... shall be spent on the work by the contractor. Any portion of this sum not spent shall be refunded by the contractor.

3.03 Materials and Workmanship: Materials shall be new and of stated quality. Workmanship shall be of the best quality.

3.04 Plants: Plants shall be of an average minimum retail value of $5.

3.05 Insurance .... who's responsible.

3.06 Damage .... who's responsible.

3.07 Payment .... detail of method of payment.

3.08 Maintenance .... if applicable, who does what.

4. SCOPE

This section details exactly what the work does and does not include (e.g. supply, delivery, installation, planting, watering etc.)

5. WORK

If relevant, this section can be included to detail work to be done by persons other than the landscape contractor (sub-contractors). Sections might be included for plumbers, carpenters, concreters, etc.

Know your work inside out before starting to put together a specification.

Appendix

DISTANCE EDUCATION COURSES

The authors of this book conduct a wide variety of correspondence courses through the Australian Correspondence Schools. Courses range from short courses requiring around 80 to 100 hours of study, up to Certificate Courses (600 hours), Advanced Certificates (700 hours) and Advanced Diplomas (2550 hours). All courses are conducted via correspondence, with no classroom time required, so are flexible enough to fit into a busy schedule, especially for those just starting a new business.

Short courses

Most short courses can be completed in 3 to 4 months or, if study time is limited, can take up to 12 months. Short courses particularly relevant to those wanting to start a landscape or garden business include:

Business
Starting a Small Business, Project Management, Marketing, Business Operations

Landscape design
Cottage Garden Design, Bush Garden Design, Park and Playground Design, Landscaping 1 and 2.

Garden maintenance
Soil Management, Plant Protection, Weed Control and Identification, Irrigation, Horticultural Management, Horticulture 1, 2 and 3.

Turf care
Sports Turf Management, Turf Repair and Renovation, Turf Care
   Plus many more!

CERTIFICATE, ADVANCED CERTIFICATE AND ADVANCED DIPLOMA COURSES

Certificate in Horticulture (C12CN002)
A 600 hour course—300 hours involving general horticultural studies and a further 300 hours in any one of 15 different specialisations. Options to specialise include: Landscaping, Turf, Ornamental Horticulture, Arboriculture and Plant Protection.

Advanced Certificate in Applied Management (C12CN001)
A 700 hour course which develops both business management and horticultural skills. Areas of specialisation include Retail Nursery, Wholesale Nursery and Horticultural Technology.

Advanced Diploma in Horticulture (C12CN004)
An accredited and nationally recognised qualification, taking 3 years full time or 5–7 years part time. This course consists of 21 modules plus a variety of workshops, seminars and research projects. Course work includes Biochemistry, Computer Studies, Business Studies, Instructional Skills, Workplace Health and Safety plus 8 units in your chosen area of study and 8 elective units.

VIDEOS

The Australian Correspondence Schools also produce a range of educational videos which can be helpful to people in the landscape and gardening industry. Titles include:

> Designing a Garden
> Herb Identification
> Plant Identification
> Australian Native Plants
> Plant Propagation

Further information on the school and its services, including fees and enrolment information, can be obtained from:
A.C.S. 264 Swansea Rd Lilydale, 3140 Ph: (03) 9736 1882 Fax: (03) 9736 4034
    or
P.O. Box 2092 Nerang East, Qld. 4211. Ph: (07) 5530 4855 Fax: (07) 5525 1728
    website http://www.acs.edu.au
    E mail   admin@acs.edu.au
    ACS GARDENING WEBSITE   http://www.acs.edu.au/hort
    ACS BUSINESS WEB SITE   http://www.acs.edu.au/bus

FOR MORE INFORMATION

Other books by John Mason

John Mason has published a wide range of books on horticulture, agriculture and related topics. Here a few of the titles that may be of most assistance to those starting up a landscape or gardening business.

• *Growing Tropical Plants* • *Growing Australian Natives* • *Growing Ferns* •
Starting a Nursery or Herb Farm • *Nursery Management*

The Internet

The Internet is quickly becoming an important source of information in all areas of business and interest. While some sites are available to users over the long term, many change very quickly, via change of address, change of supplier, etc. Often you can get in contact with a specific business just by typing in the business name. For example http://www.scottslawn.com will give you access to Scotts Lawn Company, an international supplier of fertiliser and turf products.

Listed here are some websites, operational at the time of publication, which we think you may find useful in getting information.

Landscape and Gardening

Environment Centre	http://www.iinet.net.au/~ecwa/info
Institute of Horticulture UK	http://www.horticulture.demon.co.uk
Wild Dog Gardening Books	http://www.gsat.edu.au/~users/wildog
The Arbor Age	http://www.arborists.com
Australian Gardening Magazine	http://www.global-garden.com.au
CSIRO	http://www.dwr.csiro.au

Small business

The Business Forum Online www.businessforum.com/bookmarks.html
A good source of information on books and training available, as well as access to some prime academic centres in the United States. Also has a great deal of information on US tax laws, legislation, etc.

Small and Home Based Business Links www.bizoffice.com /index.html
A good place to start to source other contacts on information for small businesses and home-based business. Includes information on services, marketing and franchise opportunities.

Guide to Australia www.csu.edu.au/australia
Excellent site, full of material needed to begin market research. Gives details and run down of Australian demographics, both nationally and on a state-by-state basis.

USEFUL CONTACTS

For information, advice, publications, conferences, to join, to meet colleagues, or simply to learn more about your new industry.

Associations

INSTITUTE OF HORTICULTURE
A British based organisation serving professional horticulturists throughout the world.
80 Vincent Square, London, SW1P 2PE, U.K.

AUSTRALIAN INSTITUTE OF HORTICULTURE
15 Bowen Cres, West Gosford, NSW, 2250
Phone: (02) 4325 4088

AUSTRALIAN TURFGRASS RESEARCH INSTITUTE
Provides research, information and Advisory services
P.O. Box 190, Concord West, NSW, 2183
Phone: (02) 9736 1223

AUSTRALIAN GOLF COURSE SUPERINTENDENTS ASSOCIATION
Suite 10A, 3 Chester St, Oakleigh Vic. 3166
Phone: (03) 9563 4777

ARBORICULTURAL ASSOCIATION
Ampfield House, Ampfield, nr Romsey, Hants, SO51 9PA, U.K.
Phone: 01794 368717

LANDSCAPE CONTRACTORS ASSOCIATION OF NSW LTD.
PO Box 1226, Bankstown, NSW, 2200
Ph:(02) 9790 5151, Fax: (02) 9796 2726.

LANDSCAPE INDUSTRIES ASSOCIATION OF VICTORIA
PO Box 218, Mentone, 3194 Vic.
Ph: (03) 9587 8511

AUSTRALIAN INSTITUTE OF LANDSCAPE ARCHITECTS
P.O. Box 1646, ACT, 2601.
Phone: (02) 6248 9970

BRITISH ASSOCIATION OF LANDSCAPE INDUSTRIES
9 Henry St, Keighley, West Yorkshire, BD21 3DR U.K.

LANDSCAPE INSTITUTE
6–8 Barnard Mews, London, SW11 1QU, U.K.
Phone: 0171 738 916

AMERICAN HORTICULTURAL SOCIETY
7931 East Boulevard Dr., Alexandria, Virginia 22308–1300 USA
Phone: (800) 777 7931

SOUTHERN NURSERYMEN'S ASSOCIATION (USA)
1000 Johnson Ferry Rd., Suite E–130, Marietta, Georgia, 36068 USA
Phone: (770) 973 9026

WESTERN ASSOCIATION OF NURSERYMEN (USA)
23750 State Route V, Clarksdale, Missouri 00430 USA
Phone: (816) 369 3115

Publications

AUSTRALIAN HORTICULTURE
TURF CRAFT INTERNATIONAL
Rural Press Magazines, PO Box 160,
Port Melbourne, Vic.
Ph:(03) 9287 0900

LANDSCAPE AUSTRALIA
Landscape Publications, PO box 356,
Mont Albert, Vic. Ph: (03) 9890 5764

GOLF & SPORTS TURF AUSTRALIA
POWER EQUIPMENT AUSTRALIA
Glenvale Publication, PO Box 347,
Glen Waverly, Vic. Ph: (03) 9544 2233

AUSTRALIAN GARDEN GUIDE
THE GREEN LEAF GARDENING
SERIES
Express Publications, 2 Stanley St.
Silverwater, NSW. Ph: (02) 9748 0599

Small business information

There are a great many books, publications and advisory services dealing with
the small and micro-business sectors (micro-businesses generally being those
employing fewer than 5 people). While each type of business has its individual
needs and challenges, the general information provided from these sources makes
a good starting point for subjects such as marketing, selling techniques,
bookkeeping, etc.

Listed here are the Small Business Advisory services for each state and
territory in Australia. They are a good starting point for finding out what
information is available and also for any government assistance that may be
available for the new business owner.

ACT
Business Link
12a Thesiger Court, Deakin
PO Box 192 Deakin ACT 2600
Ph:(02) 6283 5200 Fax: (02) 6282 2436

NEW SOUTH WALES
Dept. of Business & Regional Dev.
3rd Flr., 1 Fitzwilliam St.,Parramatta
PO Box 242, Parramatta NSW 2124
Ph:(02)9242 6700 Fax:(02) 9242 6707

NORTHERN TERRITORY
Territory Business Centre
Development House, 76 The
Esplanade, Darwin
PO Box 4160, Darwin NT 0801
Ph:(08) 8999 7916 Fax:(08) 8999 7924

QUEENSLAND
Dept. of Tourism, Small Business &
Industry
21st Flr, 111 George St., Brisbane
GPO Box 1141, Brisbane, QLD 4001
Ph:(07) 3405 6789 Fax:(07) 3225 2443

SOUTH AUSTRALIA
The Business Centre
145 South Terrace, Adelaide
GPO Box 1565, Adelaide SA 5001
Ph: (08) 8233 4600 Fax: (08) 8231 1199

TASMANIA
Tasmania Development & Resources
5th Flr. ANZ Building, 22 Elizabeth
St., Hobart
PO Box 646 Hobart Tas. 7001
Ph: (03) 6233 5712 Fax: (03) 6233 5800

VICTORIA
Small Business Victoria
Lev. 5, 55 Collins St, Melbourne 3000
Ph· (03) 9651 9888 Fax: (03) 9651 9725
Toll Free: 1 800 136 034

WESTERN AUSTRALIA
Small Business Development
Corporation
553 Hay St., Perth
GPO Box C111, Perth, WA 6001
Ph: 1 800 093 340 Fax: (08) 9221 1132

Index